MUSICAL iPAD®

quick PRO guides

MUSICAL iPAD®

Performing, Creating, and Learning Music on Your iPad®

Thomas Rudolph
and Vincent Leonard

Hal Leonard Books
An Imprint of Hal Leonard Corporation

Published in 2014 by Hal Leonard Books
An Imprint of Hal Leonard Corporation
7777 West Bluemound Road
Milwaukee, WI 53213

Trade Book Division Editorial Offices
33 Plymouth St., Montclair, NJ 07042

Printed in the United States of America

Book design by Adam Fulrath
Book composition by Kristina Rolander

Library of Congress Cataloging-in-Publication Data is available upon request.

ISBN 978-1-4803-4244-6

www.halleonardbooks.com

To the memory of my father,
Sylvester J. Rudolph, who until his dying day was still
amazed I could write not one, but many, books
—Thomas Rudolph

To the memory of
Maureen Smakulski and Thomas Leonard
—Vincent Leonard

Contents

Chapter 2

Chapter 3

FOREWORD

From the authors that have provided us with such great books on Finale, Sibelius, and recording techniques, *Musical iPad* is a comprehensive approach to learning and making music on Apple's popular tablet device. This book will help you learn the most appropriate ways to configure the iPad for music creation and connect it to other musical devices, and suggest powerful apps for all your musical needs.

Tom Rudolph and Vince Leonard are educators and authors of great distinction. They have the ability to take complex concepts and break them down into simpler components, explain what these concepts mean in easy-to-understand language, show you how to use them in real-world situations with practical applications, and demonstrate how all of this can help make you a better musician and how to better express yourself creatively with today's technology tools.

With the release of the iPad, Apple has brought yet another major new tool for creative exploration and expression to the world market. Although it is a very easy-to-use device, finding the "right" apps has become increasingly difficult with the many options available in the iTunes App Store, and connecting the iPad to music-making devices such as keyboards, MIDI and audio interfaces, and sound systems is not well outlined or explained in Apple's documentation. Tom and Vince to the rescue with this book!

Musical iPad will help you turn your mobile device into a powerful amplifier for your creativity—and turn your modest investment in a tablet device into an extremely valuable tool for learning and making music. The well-written, easy-to-follow instructions and descriptions will get you up to speed in no time and will help you make the most of your Apple iPad.

DAVID MASH
Senior Vice President for Innovation, Strategy, and Technology
Berklee College of Music

Introduction

This book is meant to be a resource for using the iPad in music and music education. It guides you step by step through the most popular and productive music apps for the iPad 2, iPad (third or fourth generation), or iPad mini. *Musical iPad* provides guidance for using the best iPad music apps and demonstrates how to apply them in your musical life. The book does not include all of the iPad music apps. Rather, it focuses on apps that run on the iPad self-contained as opposed to apps that are meant to control external music gear. That's the topic for a future book.

It is not an attempt to address all of the current music applications, but rather to highlight and organize them into the most popular ways to use the iPad in music and music education and describe the most popular apps.

This book is designed for both novice and experienced iPad users. If you are a beginner iPad user, we suggest you start with chapter 1 and proceed sequentially through the text. If you have a specific need, then peruse the chapters as needed. You may want to take advantage of the e-book version so you can read it right on your iPad.

Companion Website

The book is only part of the learning experience. Each chapter includes links to video demonstrations of apps and the chapter activities. Also, the website will keep current with new apps that come into the market. You will want to visit the website frequently.

For those of you who purchased the print version of this book, the video tutorials have a QR code printed. These look like:

Figure 0.1. Hal Leonard website: www.halleonardbooks.com/ebookmedia/119292

You can use your smartphone or your iPad to read the codes to take you directly to the link. If you don't have an installed QR code reader, you can download one from iTunes.

Quick Scan QR Code Reader by iHandy Inc. (Free)

https://itunes.apple.com/us/app/quick-scan-qr-code-reader/id483336864?mt=8

We welcome your feedback. Please feel free to contact us with your comments: Tom Rudolph (tom@tomrudolph.com) and Vince Leonard (vince@vinceleonard.com).

ACKNOWLEDGMENTS

The authors, Tom Rudolph and Vince Leonard, would like to thank the following individuals for their help and assistance with this publication:

Liia Rudolph for her astute edits and content suggestions, Alex Gittelman for his suggestions about specific music apps and his video interviews.

John Cerullo, Bill Gibson, David Mash, Susan Basalik, David Fair, Arthur Roolfs, John Dunphy, George Pinchock, Lauri Leonard, Carole Kriessman, and David Hawley for their help and assistance.

Musical iPad®

Chapter 1
Getting Started

This chapter is an introduction for readers unfamiliar with the basics of the iPad. If you are familiar with the iPad and its operation, you are welcome to scan the contents of this chapter and move on to chapter 2.

The First Post-PC Device: Tool or Toy?

When the iPad launched in August of 2010, it created a new type of mobile device: the tablet computer. This combines the portability of a smartphone with a screen size close to a small laptop. Though initially criticized as nothing more than a large iPod Touch, Apple's music and game-oriented version of the iPhone, the larger screen provided software developers with more options than the limited screen size of a smartphone such as the iPhone.

Since the iPad and the iPhone share the same brain or operating system, the iPad can run the applications already created for the iPhone. With new apps designed specifically for the larger iPad screen, there quickly became so many apps that books like this are needed to get through all of the options.

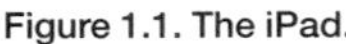
Figure 1.1. The iPad.

Music Friendly

With the iPad continuing to be more and more popular, the software and hardware add-ons for music hobbyists, students, teachers, and musicians are growing at a rapid pace. The iPad has established itself not as a toy but as a serious productive tool. For the music studio performer, it's an external controller for studio hardware and software, as well as a synthesizer or sampler. For performing musicians, it can be a tuner, metronome, music folder, and effects rack. For songwriters, it is a sketch pad and portable studio. On gigs, it can help with mixing and recording the concert. But yes, you can also use it for playing games and checking your e-mail.

iPad Dimensions

The iPad is smaller than a piece of letter-sized paper and thinner than a book. Its external controls are simple:

- A power button on the top.
- Two volume controls on the right side.
- A switch that can alternately mute audio or lock the orientation to portrait or landscape.
- A single button on the bottom, located in the center below the screen.

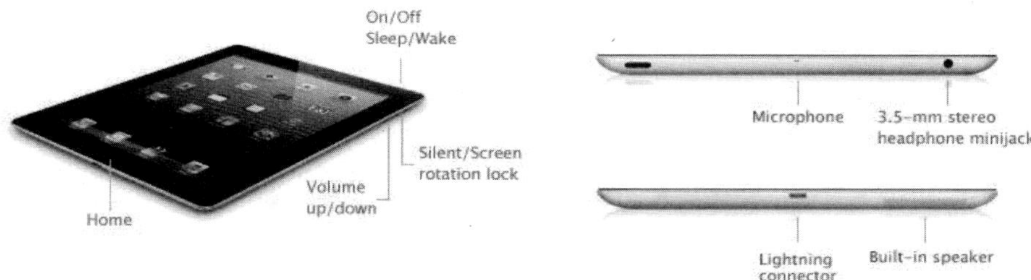

Figure 1.2. iPad controls.

All iPads since the iPad 2 have two cameras: one on the upper-left corner of the back and another that is centered in the border above the screen. There are two ports: a stereo mini headphone jack on the top left and a port on the bottom. It is powered by a rechargeable battery, and it can be charged by plugging its docking cable into a computer's USB port or into its power adapter. To operate it, all you need is your finger. Press the power button on top of the screen, and the iPad comes to life. For those familiar with the iPhone, the iPad works in a similar manner, only larger.

The iPad experience is all about the larger screen size. When smartphones were launched, it was cool to watch TV shows or movies on a phone, but on the iPad you now can actually see the details on the screen. The same can be said for computer-game interfaces; more room allows for more attention to detail. The iPad is easily portable, and anyone (including my mom) can learn to use it in minutes.

iOS

The operating system for the iPad—the software it uses to perform its basic functions—is called iOS. The "i" was first used by Apple when it introduced the iMac in 1998, and back then the "i" stood for Internet. Now Apple uses the "i" with many of their products: iPhone, iPod, iTunes, iBooks, and software suites iWork and iLife. The letters *OS* stand for operating system. So iOS is the Apple operating system that is used on Apple's mobile devices, including the iPhone and iPad.

Apple continues to update the iOS, and every time they do, they add a number to it, such as iOS5, iOS6, and so forth. It is usually a good idea to install the latest version of the operating system.

Once the iPad is activated, the Home screen with a background photo and neatly arranged icons appear.

Each icon represents an "app," or application, that is installed on the iPad. The icon positions are fixed by the operating system in five rows of four in portrait orientation, or four rows of five in landscape.

Figure1.3. iPad Home screen.

> **Tip:** A page or image displayed in portrait mode is taller than it is wide. A page or image displayed in landscape mode is wider than it is tall.

It is possible to change icon placement, but that position still must conform to the grid. It is also possible to arrange your apps using your computer's iTunes application while the iPad is attached to your computer via cable. Along the bottom of the screen, there is a dock with four icons across it. There is room on the doc to add two more icons for a total of six. When the number of apps exceeds the number of spaces on the first Home screen, an additional Home screen is created. The dock and its icons are always at the bottom of any Home screen. A row of white dots just above the dock icons indicates the number of Home pages on your iPad. Navigation between multiple Home screens is done by dragging or flicking a single finger across the screen. A right-to-left motion will move to the next Home screen to the right. Conversely, a left-to-right motion will move to the next Home screen to the left. To the left of the first Home screen is the Search window in iOS 6 or earlier; in iOS7 swipe from top to bottom.

VIDEO 1.1. IPAD APP ORGANIZATION.

Figure 1.4.
http://youtu.be/QGg53XYneMY

Searches can include apps, contacts, podcasts, videos, notes, events in the calendar, reminders, messages, songs in iTunes, and the senders, recipients, and subject lines of e-mail documents. Mac computer users will find this feature similar to Spotlight on OSX computers. Search is limited to the iPad and does not search a network or the Web; however, at the bottom of the search results list, there are options to search the Web using Safari, a web browsing app, or Wikipedia on Safari. The iPad will enter the same search word(s) in the search field of the browser or Wikipedia, and the results will appear immediately.

What's an App?

I'm sure you've heard the phrase "There's an app for that." The word *app* is an abbreviation of "application," which refers to a program that runs on a computer or other device. I'm writing this text on a word processor application. These include programs or applications such as Microsoft Word and Apple Pages. Applications usually refer to programs that run on a Mac or Windows computer. The term *app* or *mobile app* is used to describe programs that run on mobile devices such as the iPhone and other smartphones, and the iPad and other tablet technologies produced by other companies.

The concept of an app was first introduced with the iPhone, Apple's smartphone. Software developers create applications for the iPhone using Apple's iOS. They then post the apps to Apple's "App Store," to be purchased by anyone with an iPhone. The instant popularity of the iPhone took the app industry along with it. Apps can be created by almost anyone, and the cost is minimal when compared to computer-based software for Macs and PCs.

Figure 1.5. The App Store app.

Music, Music, Music

Music is a big part of the iPhone, because the iPhone can also be used as an iPod to listen to music. As music apps were created, musicians, hobbyists, and educators found the iPhone to be an indispensable music tool. Fast-forward to the introduction of the iPad. The iPad uses the same operating system as the iPhone, so all of the apps created for the iPhone work on the iPad.

Tip: iPhone apps on the iPad can be run in normal size in the center of the iPad's larger screen or enlarged by pressing the 2X button in the bottom-right corner of the screen. This magnifies the screen but at the original iPhone-sized screen resolution.

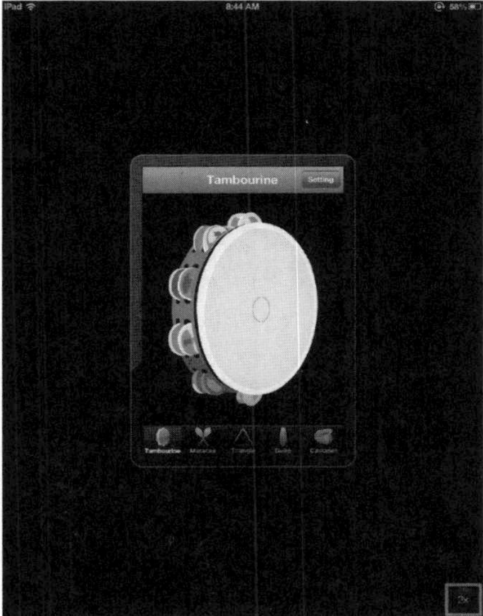

Figure 1.6. iPhone app running on an iPad.

Developers would soon revamp their products and create new ones to find innovative ways to utilize the increased iPad screen space.

Native App

With computers, if you have a Windows computer and you want to run Microsoft Word or any other program, you must purchase the version that is written to run on that computer's operating system. If you want to use Microsoft Word on a Mac, you have to purchase the Mac version. In other words, there are applications that are "native" to each computer's operating system.

The same is true with smartphones and other devices such as the iPad. Each of these devices has a unique operating system, or OS. Some include iOS (Apple devices), Android, BlackBerry, Windows Phone, WebOS and others. The iOS operating system was developed by Apple and is used to run iPhones and iPads.

Just as Microsoft makes two versions of their software for Mac and Windows, so do developers of mobile apps often create several versions so they can run on multiple mobile devices made by different manufacturers.

App Store

An app store or "applications marketplace" is usually created and maintained by a specific vendor such as Apple, Google, Intuit, and others. As an iPad user, you will be purchasing your apps from the Apple App Store. The App Store sells apps for all Apple products, including Apple computers, iPhones, and iPads.

> **Tip:** Starting with Apple's Mountain Lion operating system, the App Store has been built into the Apple operating system. This makes purchasing and installing apps a snap, and you can purchase apps via your computer or iPad.

The App Store makes it easy to search for and read reviews of apps that you are considering adding to your device(s). When you search for apps in the App Store, you can read about the application, as well as reviews posted by other users.

The price of mobile apps is usually free or very inexpensive. The prices of apps are usually under $5. Thus, adding apps to your device won't break the bank.

You can view the App Store on a computer or on your iPad or iPhone. If you are on a computer, point your web browser to www.apple.com/osx/apps/app-store.html.

On an iPhone or iPad, launch the App Store app (see Fig. 1.5).

Managing Document Files in iOS

There is one major difference with iOS devices such as the iPhone or iPad when compared to Mac and PC computers. Namely, with iOS devices, the files associated with an app are not visible, as they are on computers in document folders and the like. iOS keeps all related files hidden, accessible only by running the app.

For example, if you purchase a song on iTunes, it will only be visible and accessible after launching iTunes. Download a movie, and it will only be visible and accessible by first launching Videos. Even the text documents created by the app Pages, Apple's word processing program, are only revealed after launching the app.

Managing documents is handled in several ways. All of Apple's apps are now cloud based, so a file created in Pages is automatically synched with Apple's iCloud service. Once stored in Apple's iCloud service, it can be accessed by any computer or iOS device synched to your account. The document can be archived by saving it to computer and storing it on a backup drive or writeable media. The cloud is described later in this chapter.

Transferring Files via iTunes

Documents can also be transferred to and from the iPad using iTunes. For this process, the device must be connected to your computer using the 30-pin or Lightning cable. Select your iPad as the device, select the Apps tab, and scroll down to File Sharing at the bottom of the Apps screen to manage all of the documents that can be transferred to and from the iPad. Only apps capable of creating and loading files will be listed here.

Figure 1.7. Apple iTunes.

VIDEO 1.2. MANAGING FILES AND APPS WITH ITUNES.

Figure 1.8.
http://youtu.be/jMirahyldmo

The Cloud

Throughout the chapters that follow, there will be mention of cloud applications such as Dropbox, iCloud, Google Drive, and others. The cloud, or "cloud computing," received its name from the use of a cloud-shaped symbol to help you understand the complex nature of the technology. Cloud computing uses remote services such as computer file servers, usually on the Internet, where a user can store data, software, and other files.

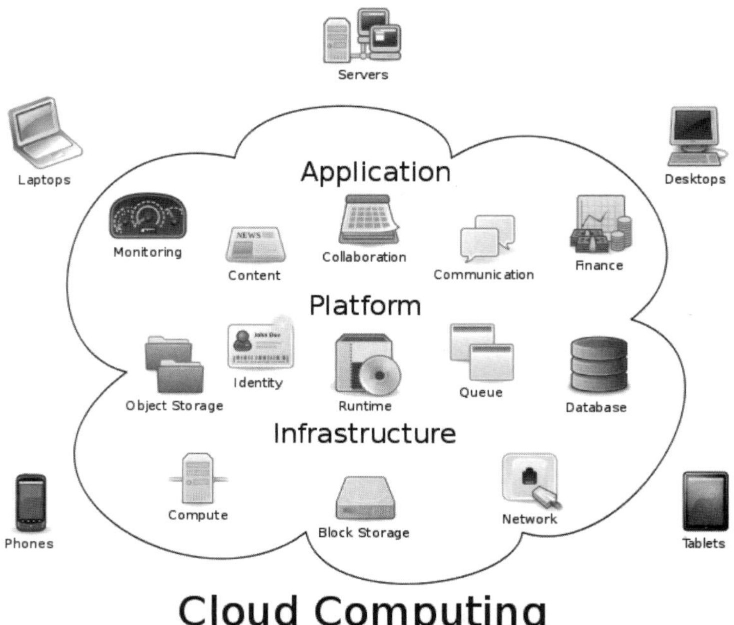

Figure 1.9. Cloud Computing.

For musicians and for the sharing of files in this book, services that allow for the posting and sharing of individual files are the best option. These include Dropbox, Google Drive, and Evernote, as well as others.

Cost: Free (Almost)

All of these services share a common format. They offer a limited amount of storage for free. When you exceed the initial storage capacity, you have a couple of options: delete files from your account or sign up for a paid option that provides more storage space.

I use several services, including Google Drive, Dropbox, and SoundCloud. Each has its own advantages and disadvantages. However, for the purpose of storing files for music that we will cover in the chapters that follow, a file-storage option is something that will save you time.

Dropbox

Dropbox users can transfer files to and from an iOS device and share these files with others. Install the Dropbox app and log into your account; then select a specific file and tap the (symbol) icon on the far right side of the menu bar, and select Open In and the application.

Figure 1.10. Dropbox.

The main advantage of storing files in the cloud is that you can access them from your computer, smartphone, or iPad, so long as you have a connection to the Internet. You can post files from all of these devices, and you can share files with others. Before selecting your service, check to see what they offer. Some important questions to ask:

- How much free storage is made available?
- How much will it cost for additional storage?
- How easy is it to share posted files with others and your other applications?

Your account is set up on one of these services and uses a password for access. Your information and data are as safe as with services such as Facebook, Twitter, and other online accounts.

VIDEO 1.3. STORING FILES WITH DROPBOX.

Figure 1.11.
http://youtu.be/BQT0bOoJ3as

Apple's iCloud

Just like Apple's mantra "Think different," their cloud service, called iCloud, is not the same as the other services described earlier in this chapter. The difference with iCloud is it works in the background and syncs files from your devices: iPad, iPhone, and computer. The operating system of the device actually does the synching for you. Unlike Dropbox or other services, there are no folders, and you can't drag a file to iCloud and then share it with others manually.

I use iCloud as a backup for certain aspects of the devices I use. It is indispensable when you set up a calendar, and then you can see any changes made on other devices. It works like this:

- Set up iCloud as the cloud service for some or all of the documents and shared items, such as calendars on all of your devices.
- When you change something on a document or calendar, it is automatically sent to your iCloud account without you needing to do anything manually, so long as you are connected to the Internet.

Apple's iCloud does have a place to help you back up and share files. However, for storing specific files for use on your iPad and other devices, going with a service such as Dropbox or Google Drive is a better option.

Networking

The iPad is designed to be a wireless device. It can download e-mail and attached files, apps, music, video, and OS updates without being tethered to a computer or Internet router. Wireless communication is very powerful and versatile, but not without its share of potential problems. One tiny gap in communication from iPad to device may result in the link being lost, requiring a manual reset. The same may occur when an app stops working, referred to as a crash. This can be a liability, so it is good to have a backup plan ready to go at a moment's notice.

iPad Accessories

When I purchased my first iPad, I ended up spending another $200 or so on accessories, some of which are really helpful. These can be organized into the categories seen below.

Apple Accessories

There are accessories that Apple produces for the iPad. These include a cover, dock, and wireless keyboard. You can purchase these when you order your iPad or after the purchase: www.apple.com/ipad/accessories/.

iPad Smart Cover

I highly recommend the iPad Smart Cover. It is excellent for protecting the iPad, and it can be used to adjust the viewing angle.

iPad Dock

The iPad docking station gives you a personal hub, which, when connected, gives you access to a port for synching or charging and an audio line out port for connecting to powered speakers via an optional audio cable.

Apple Wireless Keyboard

This typing keyboard uses Bluetooth technology, so it can be used with computers and your iPad. This gives you a physical typing service that can be used with your iPad. If you do a lot of typing on the iPad, this is a valuable accessory to invest in.

Third-Party Accessories

Third party refers to companies that are not part of the manufacturer but supply materials for the device. There are many companies that specialize in creating innovative products for the iPad, including cases, external keyboards, and more.

Cases

You've made a big investment in your iPad, so it makes sense to get a good case, just as you would with your other musical hardware and instruments. You can purchase a carrying case for the iPad such as those made by OtterBox (www.otterbox.com) and Hard Candy Cases (www.hardcandycases.com).

I am pleased with the Hard Candy carrying case. Expect to pay $50 or more for a solid carrying case.

Cases with Typing Keyboards

Another option is to use a case and QWERTY keyboard combination. As with other accessories, there are a host from which to choose. The Logitech Keyboard Case by ZAGG for the iPad includes a carrying case and a physical typing keyboard: www.zagg.com/accessories/logitech-ipad-2-keyboard-case. Other options include the Kensington Keyfolio: www.kensington.com/kensington/us/us/s/1615/keyboard-folio-cases.aspx.

If you do a lot of typing, this is something you will want to add. These combo cases and keyboards are priced in the $75 to $125 range.

Hardware Cautions and Software Caveats

While exploring the brave new world of iPad software development can be exciting, the digital frontier can be a cold place if you are not careful. Take this "authorly" advice with you as you browse.

Memory

As with any computer, the amount of internal memory is important, and getting the iPad with the highest internal storage capacity will allow you to work longer. So if you are purchasing an iPad or considering upgrading to a new one, choose the model with the most memory you can afford. The more the better. The iPad's memory isn't expandable, so be sure to purchase the memory you need. The current memory options are 16 GB, 32 GB, 64 GB, and 128 GB: http://store.apple.com/us/buy/home/shop_ipad/family/ipad?product=IPAD2012-4GEN_MAIN.

App Developers

The majority of software in the iTunes store is created by smaller companies compared to the names we are familiar with from desktop computer applications. These small companies may be single-person shops or small groups of people, possibly working together from different locations. App development may not be their principle gig, so don't expect the same tech-support experience as with a larger company. A small developer may have to make a difficult choice between time spent fixing a software bug or communicating with a user base that is clamoring for an upgrade, so you may need a bit more patience if you encounter a problem. Yes, you should expect the product to work properly, as advertised, and let the company know if you have any problems. Check the developer's website and see if there is a tech-support blog there and look at the issues other users may be experiencing. Always read the reviews before purchasing any app, and look for the number of reviews and how recently the app was released or updated. Companies do go out of business or stop supporting unsuccessful products; when researching an app purchase, check to make sure the app you are about to purchase is not an orphan.

Chapter 1 Activities

1. Check the iOS on your iPad. Do you have the latest version? In not, install it.
2. Rearrange the icons on your iPad.
3. Connect your iPad to your computer and run iTunes. Review the process for copying files for specific apps.
4. Open an account for cloud storage with a service such as Dropbox.
5. Create a wish list of accessories you want for your iPad. Put them in priority order.

Summary

This chapter introduced the iPad and outlined how it has quickly become an integral tool for musicians, teachers, and students. The basic operation of the unit was addressed. The operating system, iOS, was described in detail. The file storage of the iPad was reviewed with reference to cloud-based computing. Apps were defined, as well as accessories to enhance the iPad experience.

Chapter 2
Music Listening and Basic Tools

This chapter will deal with ways to use your iPad to listen to music from a variety of sources and for basic musicianship tools such as an instrument tuner, metronome, and music reference guide.

Playing Music Options

When the iPad was announced to the world on January 27, 2010, Steve Jobs outlined six things that the iPad does better than a smartphone or a laptop in order to justify its existence. Number 5 on that list was listening to your music collection. In the last few years, the choices for music on the iPad have grown from simply purchasing music from iTunes to being able to stream music and listen to live radio. In this section, we will look at some options for using your iPad to listen to music.

iTunes

The mobile or iOS version of iTunes has a similar look and feel to the computer version when viewing the store to purchase music, but appearance is where the similarities end. For listening to and viewing all purchased content, there are separate apps that manage the media you download to your iPad: iOS apps, which are handled by iTunes on the computer and managed by the App Store app. This only gives you access to iOS apps, not any of the computer apps in the OSX computer App Store. When you download content from the iTunes store, iTunes will switch over to the appropriate app to view your purchase. Each app has a Store button that will switch to the iTunes app for additional browsing and purchasing.

Figure 2.1. iTunes 5. The App Store app.

So all you need to do is purchase a song, album, or movie on any of your devices—computer, iPhone, iPad. You can then access these files from any device. The storage for this is done via the cloud, as described in chapter 1.

VIDEO 2.1. ITUNES.

Figure 2.2.
http://youtu.be/X5zfNoht6iE

> **Tip:** One of my favorite features of the iTunes store is the "Single of the Week." This is a free download from a new release so listeners can take a chance on an unfamiliar artist.

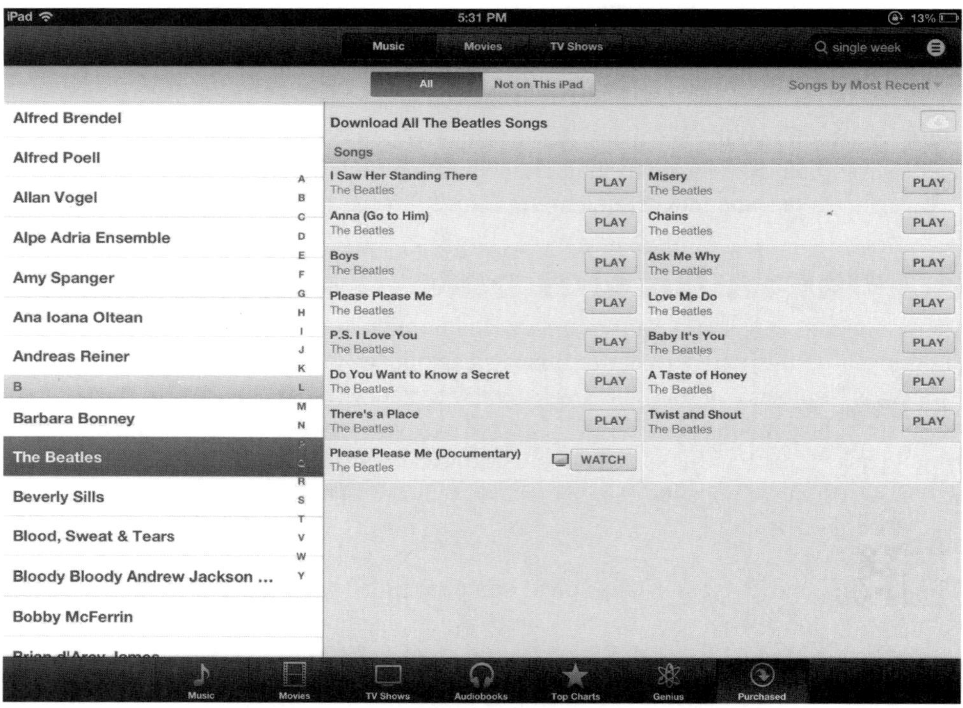

Figure 2.3. iTunes on iPad.

Figure 2.4. iPad Music App icon.

The Music App

The Music app functions as database manager and player for all the music files on your iPad. Your music collection can be viewed in several ways. The Music app will use the information encoded in the files to organize by song title, album, artist, genre, and composer, or you can create playlists to group together your own collections for any criteria you choose.

VIDEO 2.2. MUSIC APP.

Figure 2.5.
http://youtu.be/wh7gK2gjJhQ

If the iPad is the only Apple device you own, all your music will be located here as well as stored in your iCloud space, which comes free with your iPad registration. If you have a computer, and that device contains your main iTunes library, there are several ways of managing the content on your iPad. Connect the iPad to the computer via the appropriate USB connector cable, and the iPad appears as a device in the computer's iTunes app. You can then manage the content transferred to your iPad using the automatic setting or manually select which tracks are transferred to the iPad. Apple has another solution to manage music across all of your iOS devices called iTunes Match. This service has an annual fee of $24.99 but carries the bonus of giving you access to all the songs and albums in your computer's iTunes folder, even if you did not purchase the album or song at the iTunes store. Accessing the complete library at all times on your iOS device requires a Wi-Fi or wireless connection. Without that, you will only be able to play the files downloaded to your iPad.

VIDEO 2.3. ENABLING ITUNES MATCH ON THE COMPUTER AND IPAD.

Figure 2.6.
http://youtu.be/WZIWbh0vpSA

Take a minute to familiarize yourself with the options for controlling volume on the iPad. The most obvious are the two buttons located on the right side (when holding the iPad in portrait orientation) of the case. The slider button above the volume buttons is set, by default, to be the mute button. In the down position, sound is muted.

Tip: The slider button can also be set to lock the screen to a set orientation so it will not change as the iPad is moved either by unplanned jostling or as a part of game play.

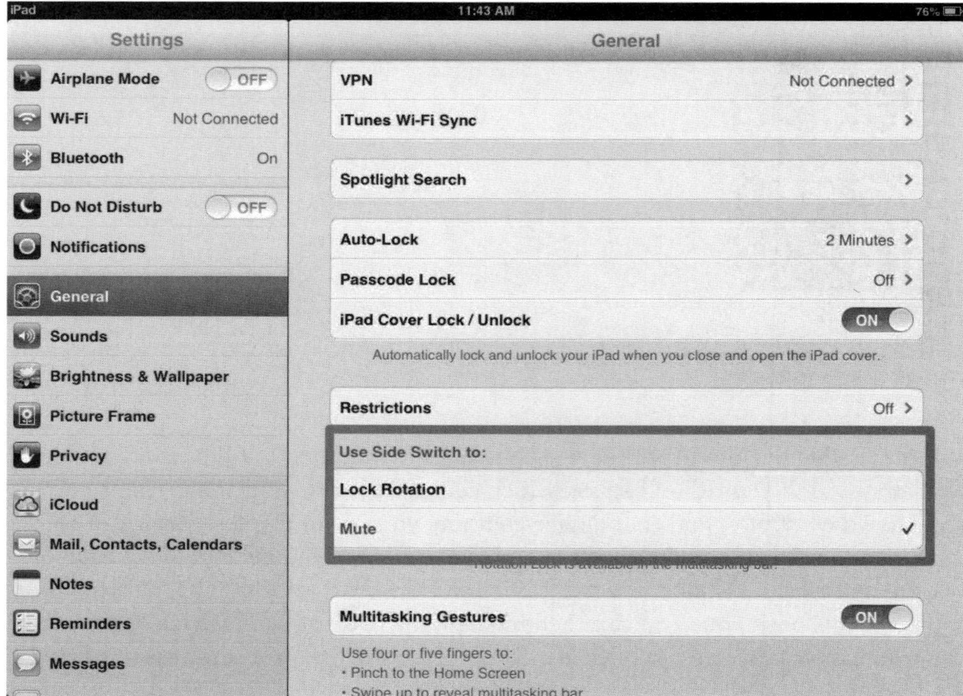

Figure 2.7. Slide Switch.

The sound controls can be accessed on the screen inside any app by double-tapping the Home button. When the row of app icons appears at the bottom of the screen, swipe left to right until the volume and transport controls appear on the screen. Tap the Home button once to return the screen to normal view.

VIDEO 2.4. ITUNES FREE CONTENT.

Figure2.7a.
http://youtu.be/dKZM9B4lZ9Y

To further explore the iTunes interface, look for a link to the "Free on iTunes" section. Here you can view free content of all types. Try downloading different types of content so you see how iTunes handles the handoff to other apps; then locate the Store button in those apps to return to the iTunes Store.

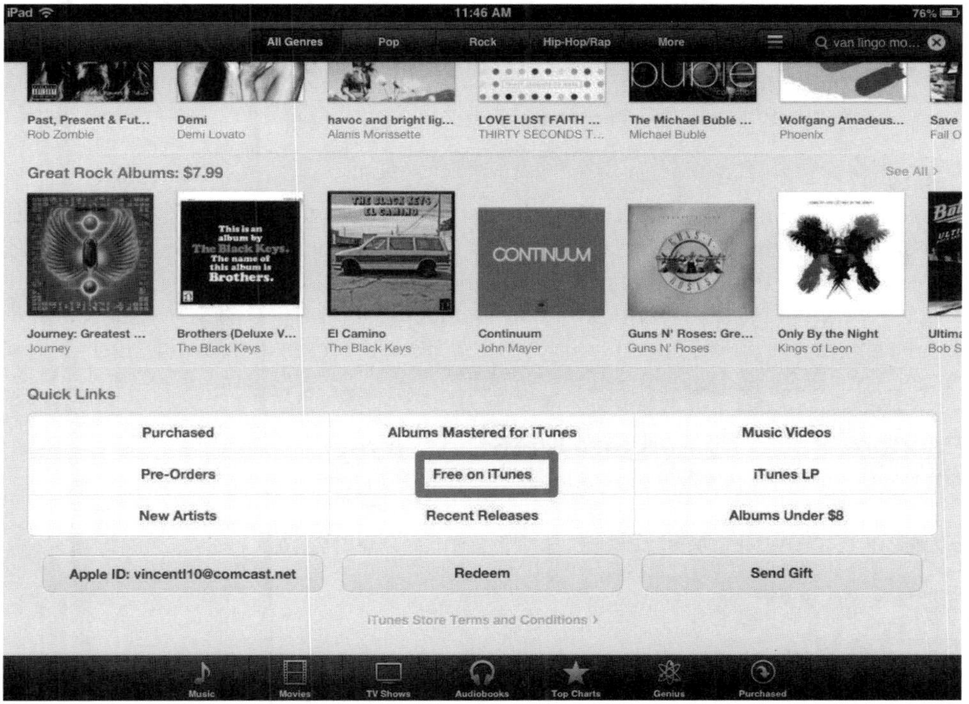

Figure 2.8. Free on iTunes button.

Music Listening Options

There are three ways to use your iPad to listen to music: you can download audio files, stream audio, and listen to Internet radio. As you move away from traditional avenues of music merchandising in an effort to discover new artists, you will find all three useful, depending on when and where you listen.

Online Music Stores

Online music stores use a pay-for-product download approach. Apple created the download model that many, most recently Amazon, have duplicated. Downloads are usually in MP3 file format, though Apple has come up with their own format to achieve a better sound quality. Downloads are yours to keep, manage, and (I strongly suggest) back up. To help with the latter, Apple and Amazon offer space in their respective clouds to store and stream files. These files can be played back on any iOS device using the Music app (iTunes) or Amazon's Cloud Player app.

eMusic, as another example, uses downloads but charges a monthly fee. You can choose from several different plans based on your consumption needs.

Be aware that not all stores will have the latest US pop and rock releases. Check out the store's content before you create an account.

Streaming Music

Music streaming services can be thought of as on-demand radio. These services stream audio over a Wi-Fi network to a proprietary app on your iOS device. Pandora and Spotify are two of the most widely known services with large catalogs and the latest releases. Both offer two levels of service: a free service with some commercial interruptions and limitations, and a monthly subscription service with no commercials and some other perks. These services allow you to customize your stream by entering artists, albums, and songs you like, and Pandora will attempt to select similar artists and music that matches these preferences. You have the ability to skip or dislike a song, and that information will be used to refine your stream. You can have multiple "stations" tailored to your mood or activities.

Pandora

Pandora is free Internet radio. Enter an artist, track, comedian, or genre, and Pandora will create a personalized station that plays the music and more like it. You can rate songs by giving thumbs-up and thumbs-down feedback, and add variety to further refine your stations, discover new music, and help Pandora play only music you like. Pandora is free, with the option to pay for additional features. Just install the Pandora app on your iPad, and you are ready to listen.

Pandora Radio by Pandora Media Inc. (Free)

https://itunes.apple.com/us/app/pandora-radio/id284035177?mt=8

VIDEO 2.5. DOWNLOADING AND SETTING UP PANDORA.

Figure 2.9.
www.youtube.com/watch?v=RjvHfaLWdvo

Spotify

In order to use Spotify on your iPad, you have to subscribe to the Premium service for $10 per month (www.spotify.com) and download the Spotify mobile app. Spotify can access and play any song in your iTunes library. You can download tracks for offline playing. The files will play for 30 days without your device linking up with Spotify to verify that you are still a Premium subscriber. Some people use Spotify as their main music source, as you can create playlists similar to iTunes. It is definitely worth considering as an addition to iTunes.

Spotify Premium by Spotify Ltd. ($10 Monthly Fee)

https://itunes.apple.com/us/app/spotify/id324684580?mt=8

Slacker and Grooveshark

Slacker and Grooveshark are both streaming services. They provide a wide variety of listening options without the need for creating an account, so you can start listening without entering any preferences, though you can enter your favorite artists, songs, and albums to create a custom-designed listening experience.

The categories in Slacker cover the basics of musical styles, including classical music and comedy, as well as categories for Fitness, Music Festivals, Countdowns, Holidays, and Special Events, such as the Grammy Awards. Slacker also offers streaming of ABC Radio with news and magazine programming, and ESPN Radio.

Both Slacker and Grooveshark allow some personalization, so you can select the shows and topics you find most interesting. They both offer a basic free service with ads in the top part of the screen and no listening limits, as well as paid subscription options ranging from monthly to annual plans.

Listeners who prefer to voyage off the beaten path and explore different approaches to the streaming model might find Songza's Music Concierge approach the right path for music to fit any activity, mood, or time of day. There are many playlists to choose from, but if you wish to create your own, that can only be done on the website, not from the app. The app is free.

Slacker Radio by Slacker Inc. (Free)
https://itunes.apple.com/us/app/slacker-radio/id298307011?mt=8

Remote for Grooveshark by Oli Kingshott ($1.99)
https://itunes.apple.com/us/app/remote-for-grooveshark/id504583704?mt=8

Radio Stations
If you want to listen to streams from actual radio stations, TuneIn Radio (free; or Pro version, $4.99) can connect you with over 70,000 radio stations from around the world. Select programming based on location, or programming choices such as music, news, talk, or sports. A map view with push pins indicates locations with available streams. The program can remember your choices for future listening. The Pro version adds the ability to record the incoming stream to your iPad for future listening.

The SiriusXM subscription service now has an iOS app, so if you already subscribe to that service, there is another option for accessing it.

SiriusXM Internet Radio by SIRIUS XM Radio Inc. (Free)
https://itunes.apple.com/us/app/siriusxm-internet-radio/id317951436?mt=8

Streaming Video
The iPad is as much about video as it is about audio, so it is just as easy to turn your iPad into a television as it is a radio. Video content can be streamed from the iTunes store, where content is purchased or rented à la carte. You can also use streaming services such as Netflix and Hulu to view videos by paying a small monthly fee to belong to the service. As good as these apps are for entertainment, the essential one for musicians is YouTube. YouTube is a free app and allows you access to the site where people post all kinds of videos, ranging from personal home movies of children or pets to how-to tutorials to cover songs to budding artists posting original music. For emerging artists, it has become a key part of any marketing plan. Since musicians are consumers as well as producers, it's also a place to look for new music. If you can't find any music you like, there are always videos of cute kittens and puppies to help you get through the day.

YouTube is also a place to look for tutorial and demonstration videos posted by many software and hardware companies in the music business, including some products you will see in this book.

Just as with the audio streaming apps, you can subscribe to channels of artists you wish to follow, and create playlists of videos you like for easy referencing.

YouTube by Google Inc. (Free)

https://itunes.apple.com/us/app/youtube/id544007664?mt=8

Figure 2.10.

Streaming Video at Home

While streaming is mostly thought of as a way of delivering content from a remote source, anyone with a large media collection on his or her home hard drive can use streaming to deliver content to an iOS device.

Air Video and StreamToMe

Air Video and StreamToMe will stream video that is not protected by non–digital rights management (DRM)–protected video from your Mac to your iOS device. Digital rights management is the technology that prevents unwanted copying of digital files. This excludes any content purchased on the iTunes store but includes podcasts and video content from other sources. There is a work-around for this that involves playing back protected content through Safari on your iOS device. StreamToMe will work with Mac and Windows. Mac users get a bonus of having iPhoto content streamed as well. StreamToMe requires some additional software to be installed on your computer to provide the sending capability to your computer.

Air Video Free—Watch your videos anywhere! by InMethod S.R.O. (Free)

https://itunes.apple.com/us/app/air-video-free-watch-your/id313056918?mt=8

StreamToMe by Matthew Gallagher ($2.99)

https://itunes.apple.com/us/app/streamtome/id325327899?mt=8

Plex

Plex also works with both Macs and PCs and has the ability to stream music as well as video and photos. With the software installed on your computer, you can access photos from iPhoto or Aperture, or stream video content from YouTube or Vimeo, a video streaming site similar to YouTube, and Revision3, a network of new media video programming. Plex cannot stream DRM-protected content.

Plex by Plex Inc. ($4.99)

https://itunes.apple.com/us/app/plex/id383457673?mt=8

The Listening Experience

This section deals with the various ways to improve the listening experience on the iPad. The iPad also has built-in speakers that have excellent sound for speech and an audio reference. However, in order to have a high-fidelity listening experience, you will need to purchase a good pair of headphones or ear buds and/or external speakers.

Tip: Ear buds fit inside your ears, and headphones cover your ears.

iPad = No Ear Buds

If you own a first- or second-generation iPad, it came with a set of ear buds for private music listening. The third-generation and later versions do not include the standard Apple ear buds. You don't need to use Apple products; you can use any ear buds or headphones with the iPad that work with any other device you use, such as a computer or iPod, so long as they have a stereo mini plug.

Figure 2.11. Stereo mini plug.

Apple Headphones

The Apple headphones are a good place to start. However, for serious music listening, you should consider upgrading to a higher-quality headphone. And if you also use or intend to use your iPad for voice communication, I recommend purchasing headphones that also include a microphone.

Apple EarPods (With Remote and Mic)

http://store.apple.com/us/product/MD827LL/A/apple-earpods-with-remote-and-mic

Apple In-Ear Headphones with Remote and Mic

http://store.apple.com/us/product/ME186LL/A/apple-in-ear-headphones-with-remote-and-mic?fnode=49

Offer better sound quality than the earpods. Of course, higher quality = more money. For a complete list of headphones that Apple offers, including those by other companies (including Dr. Dre): http://store.apple.com/nz-hed/browse/home/shop_ipod/ipod accessories/headphones.

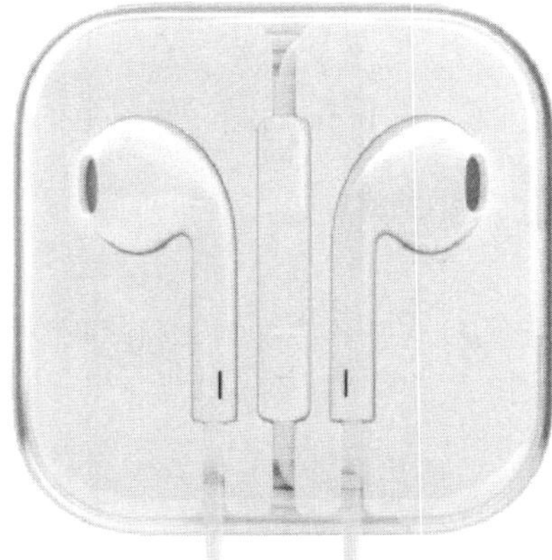

Figure 2.12. iPod accessories/headphones.

Wireless Headphones (Bluetooth)

It is possible to connect myriad devices, including earphones, to your iPad via Bluetooth technology. Devices connected via Bluetooth do not have a wire running from the headphone to the iPad. Typically these are more expensive options. Expect to pay from $250 to $750. Some of our favorites include:

- Harman Kardon Bluetooth Over-Ear Headphones ($379.00) http://store.apple.com/nz-hed/product/H8306ZM/A/harman-kardon-bluetooth-over-ear-headphones?fnode=75&p=1
- Logitech UE 9000 Wireless Bluetooth Headphones ($599) http://store.apple.com/nz-hed/product/H9883X/A/logitech-ue-9000-wireless-bluetooth-headphones?fnode=75&p=1

Figure 2.13. Harman Kardon Bluetooth Over-Ear Headphones.

External Speakers

Like headphones, there are two types of external speakers: wired and wireless. The wireless models are pricier. Since you will pay more for external speakers, I recommend listening to the sound quality before you buy them. The Apple Store and other electronic stores allow you to audition various speakers before purchasing one.

> **Tip:** A "dock" refers to a device where you plug the iPad itself right on the device. "Wired" you have to connect the speakers with a wire to the iPad's headphone jack, and "wireless" or "Bluetooth" do not need to be physically connected via wire to the iPad.

Wired External Speakers

External speakers allow you to connect speakers to the iPad. The least expensive options are those that physically connect to the iPad, either via wire or by plugging the iPad into a dock.

- The Boss Companion 2 series speakers range from $200 to $700. http://store.apple.com/nz-hed/search?find=bose+companion.

Figure 2.14. Bose® Companion® 2 Series II Multimedia Speaker System.

- The JBL OnBeat Loudspeaker Docking Station ($269) can be used with the iPad, iPod, or iPhone. The advantage is that the iPad plugs directly into the dock. http://store.apple.com/nz-hed/product/H5091X/A/jblonbeatloudspeakerdockingstation.

For the greatest variety of applications, I recommend going with an external speaker rather than a dock. With external speakers, you can still hold and use the iPad. The dock models are more for dedicated listening. Of course if you have an unlimited budget, go ahead and buy both.

Wireless (Bluetooth) Speakers

As with headphones, there are also wireless (Bluetooth) options for external speakers and docks. There are a wide range of options and price points. So again, be sure to do some listening to the speakers before purchasing.

- Harman Kardon SoundSticks Wireless Speaker System ($429). http://store.apple.com/nz-hed/product/H9442X/A/harman-kardon-soundsticks-wireless-speaker-system.
- JBL Flip Portable Bluetooth Stereo Speaker ($199) includes a built-in speaker so it can be used with FaceTime and phone calls. http://store.apple.com/nz-hed/product/HA873X/A/jbl-flip-wireless-bluetooth-speaker.

Take your time deciding which option works best for you. Getting the best sound for music listening is an important purchase regardless of whether you decide on an in- or over-ear headphone or external speakers.

Basic Tools for Musicians

The iPad can replace many stand-alone devices in your practice room, such as a tuner and metronome.

Tuner

As a trumpet player, I use several apps on my iPad regularly. The tuner not only allows me to tune my instrument, but it also lets me place the iPad next to the music on my music stand and monitor my tuning as I am playing an exercise or piece. I have used this in live performances as well.

Cleartune Chromatic Tuner by Bitcount Ltd. ($3.99)

https://itunes.apple.com/us/app/cleartune-chromatic-tuner/id286799607?mt=8

Figure 2.15.

> **Tip:** The cost of apps is refreshingly low after looking at the prices of high-end headphones and external speakers. An expensive app is one that is more than $10. However, there are some expensive apps that can replace tuners that cost many hundreds of dollars. One in this category is the TuneLab Piano Tuner designed for the professional piano tuner:
> https://itunes.apple.com/US/app/id335568329?mt=8&ign-mpt=uo%3D4.

There are many tuners on the market. Go to the App Store and search for customer reviews. In the tuner category, some musicians like to use a strobe tuner. Unlike a wheel or dial, strobe tuners show the frequency in graphic form. One option in this category is:

iChromatic Strobe Tuner HD ($4.99)

https://itunes.apple.com/US/app/id397630582?mt=8&ign-mpt=uo%3D4</BL>

VIDEO 2.6. TUNER DEMO.

Figure 2.16.
http://youtu.be/TK6NN-09m18

Pitch Pipe+ by Frozen Ape Pte. Ltd ($0.99)

https://itunes.apple.com/us/app/pitch-pipe+/id317211808?mt=8

For a cappella singing, an app to give you the starting note is needed. You can also use it to tune an instrument in a pinch.

Metronome

As with tuners, there are many metronome apps from which to choose.

Figure 2.17.

Metronome+ by Dynamic App Design ($1.99)

https://itunes.apple.com/app/metronome+/id434136233?mt=8

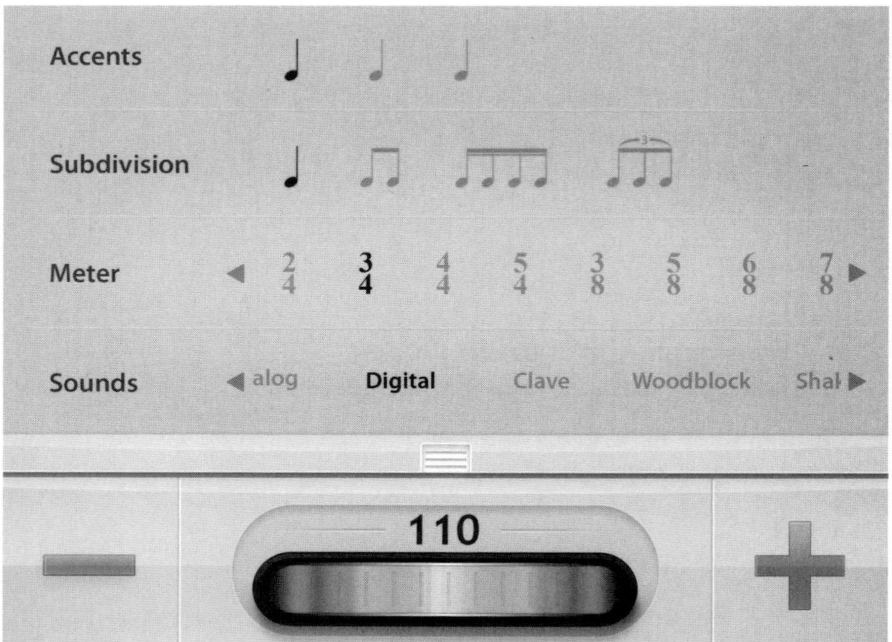

Figure 2.18.

The beauty of this app is the simple user interface and the amazing range of options for meters, accents, and the like. I use it constantly, even when I'm practicing my golf swing on the driving range: http://blog.viddler.com/cdevroe/golf-metronome/.

Ludwig Metronome by Steinway Musical Instruments (Free)

https://itunes.apple.com/us/app/ludwig-metronome/id413743609?mt=8

This free app offers a range of meters and the ability to calculate the exact number of beats per minute. This is great when you want to give a specific tempo number—just tap and watch the display to know your beats per minute, which is abbreviated BPM.

VIDEO 2.7. METRONOME DEMO.

Figure 2.19.
http://youtu.be/yDEvVWoXhqo

Chords

In chapter 6, we will cover a wide range of apps designed for music learning and education. In this chapter, we will review those apps that are designed for quick and easy reference.

ChordFinder for iPad by Codelle ($4.99)

https://itunes.apple.com/us/app/chordfinder-for-ipad/id447336937?mt=8

This app will help you search for, view, and listen to over 3,000 different chords. It is a handy reference tool and contains information about 90 different chord types in 35 different keys. You can view the notes, optional notes, and scale degrees; the various chord symbols you can encounter for each chord; and many more details.

ChordBank: Guitar Chords by WalkSoft (Free)

https://itunes.apple.com/us/app/chordbank-guitar-chords/id397602509?mt=8

Look up guitar chords with ChordBank. Full fingerings show you which fingers to put where; clearly labeled to get you up and down the fretboard.

Decibel Meter

It is a good idea to check sound levels when listening to speakers or in a live performance. Hearing damage can happen with exposure to high sound levels. A decibel meter can give you a quick reading to let you know if the sound volume is potentially hazardous to your ears. Here is a good chart for reference: www.nidcd.nih.gov/health/hearing/pages/noise.aspx.

Decibel Meter Pro by Performance Audio ($0.99)

https://itunes.apple.com/us/app/decibel-meter-pro/id382776256?mt=8

Place your iPad in any location. The built-in microphone will read the sound volumes, and they will be displayed.

Figure 2.20.

VIDEO 2.8. DECIBEL METER PRO DEMO.

Figure 2.21.
http://youtu.be/ki0APFNH_8w

Chapter 2 Activities

1. Create an iTunes playlist.
2. Enable iTunes Match on your iPad.
3. Configure one of the streaming music options, such as Spotify, Slacker, Grooveshark, or another service.
4. Connect a set of headphones or speakers to your iPad.
5. Download a tuner or metronome app, and run it on the iPad.

Summary

This chapter covered several options for playing music and video on your iPad. Options for listening using headphones and external speakers were also reviewed. The final section focused on essential apps for musicians, including a metronome, tuner, chord finder, and decibel meter.

Chapter 3
LIVE PERFORMANCE

In this chapter, you will explore how to use your iPad as a performance instrument. The categories include emulating real or acoustic instruments and music synthesis. Applications discussed can be used for personal entertainment and/or in live performance.

Software Instruments (Virtual Instruments)

The sounds that are produced by the apps discussed in this chapter are created by emulating the sounds of specific instruments. Software instruments operate entirely as software, with no physical case or box as you would have with a stand-alone electronic keyboard, acoustic piano, or other instrument. Software instruments are also called *virtual instruments*. A software synthesizer, or soft synth, is a software application that is designed to emulate some type of hardware synthesizer.

Emulating Acoustic Instruments

There are a plethora of apps to imitate acoustic and other instruments sounds. You can:

- Use an app that is designed for recording, and dial up one of the sounds it offers.
- Purchase individual apps designed to emulate a specific instrument.

Dial Up an Instrument with GarageBand

Using GarageBand for multitrack recording will be reviewed in detail in chapter 7. In this chapter, we'll focus on using GarageBand for live performance.

GarageBand by Apple (Free/In-App Purchase Upgrade $4.99)

https://itunes.apple.com/us/app/garageband/id408709785?mt=8

There are several categories of instruments that you can access with GarageBand by simply tapping the iPad screen.

GarageBand Piano

When you want to play a virtual piano, there are several keyboards from which to choose, including acoustic piano, organ, and synthesizer. The keyboard shows two octaves onscreen.

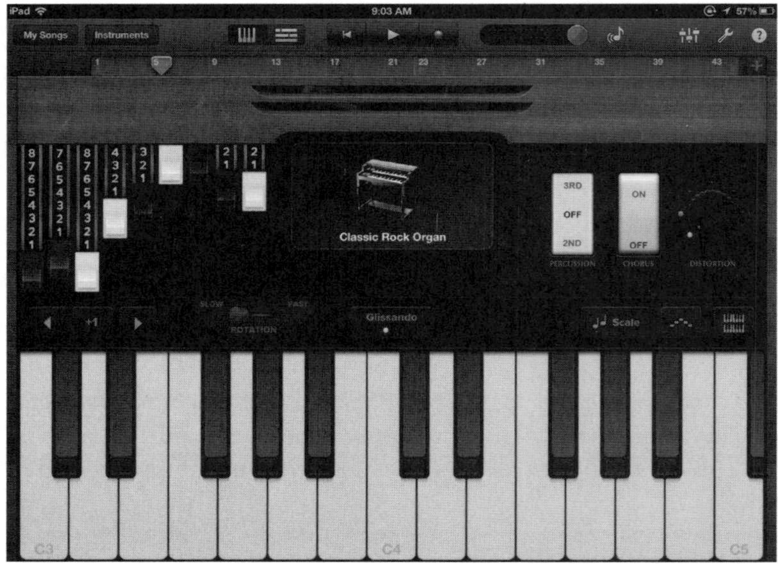

Figure 3.1. GarageBand.

There is an octave switch to move up or down, so you can, in effect, play the entire range of the acoustic piano with 88 keys. In order to help you keep track of where you are on the keyboard, GarageBand uses a system of numbers. C3 equals middle C on the acoustic piano. C4 is the octave above, and C2 is the octave below.

VIDEO 3.1. GARAGEBAND PIANO DEMO.

Figure 3.2.
http://youtu.be/C9gR9NIRaAM

Tip: You can connect a MIDI keyboard to the iPad and use it with GarageBand and many other apps. Check with your local music store or online to review your keyboard options.

Locking the Scale

There is a cool feature on GarageBand where you can "lock the scale." It defaults to C Major, but you can also select from Major, Major Pentatonic, Major Blues, Mixolydian, Klezmer, Minor Pentatonic, Minor Blues, and more.

The neat thing about this feature is that it allows you to improvise in any scale without needing to be familiar with the scale itself. For example, if you go to a jam session with a group of musicians and they start to play C Blues, you dial up C Pentatonic or Minor Blues, and you can play any note on the keyboard and sound really cool.

Smart Keyboard

GarageBand includes several smart instruments. These instruments are designed to be extra expressive. They play like their real counterparts but let you do things you could never do on a real instrument.

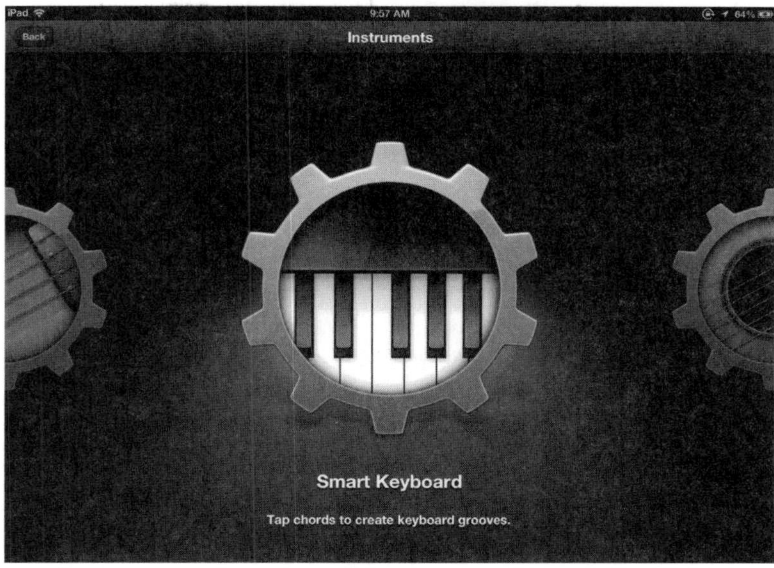

Figure 3.3. GarageBand Smart Keyboard.

When you choose the Smart Piano option, you can play a combination of single notes from chords and block chords. The chords can be played back in block or arpeggiated format. It makes for a fun environment for improvisation.

VIDEO 3.2. GARAGEBAND SMART PIANO DEMO.

Figure 3.4.
http://youtu.be/RhExyOzrwIY

Drum Set (Kit) (Tapping on a Desk on Steroids)

GarageBand offers six different drum kits. Using this app, you can easily turn drumming on a desk to jamming on a drum kit while still just tapping your fingers.

Figure 3.5. GarageBand Drum Set.

Smart Drums

Want to groove along with a beat and have your own iPad band? You can do this with the Drums or the Smart Drums. The Smart Drums are enhanced with special features you can access; for example, when you tap the snare, bass drum, toms, hi-hat, and cymbals, each produce different tones, depending on exactly where and how hard you tap them. Be sure to choose the Smart Drums rather than Drums. You can then select a random pattern by clicking the dice. Play along with the groove, and if you want, you can record the pattern and the part you improvise.

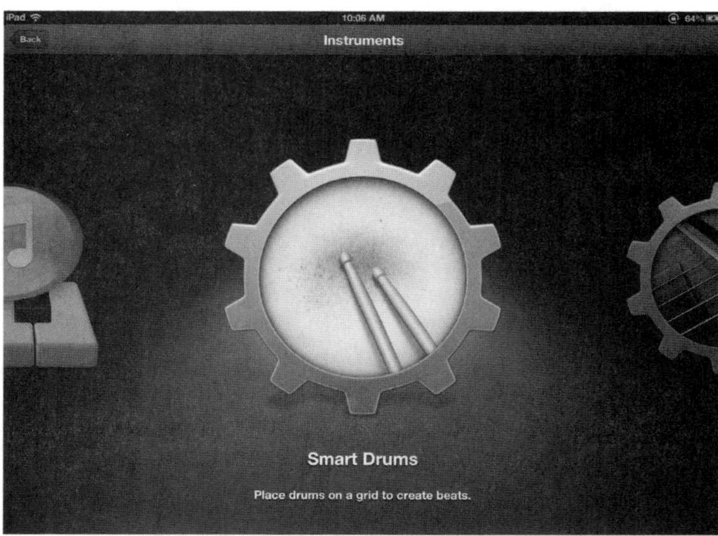

Figure 3.6. GarageBand Smart Drums.

VIDEO 3.3. GARAGEBAND SMART DRUMS DEMO.

Figure 3.7.
http://youtu.be/GW5e4KvmN-g

Guitar

There is only one option for guitar sounds in GarageBand and that's Smart Guitar. You can play the strings one note at a time and tap chords along the top of the instrument. You can choose from several guitars, including acoustic and rock. In the Smart Guitar window, you can toggle between notes or chords. And as with the piano, you can choose the scale of choice. You can easily record the parts that you play. We'll go more in depth on that in chapter 7.

> **Tip:** There is a case that facilitates holding the iPad to strum a guitar or play a piano: the HandyShell for iPad by Speck Products. Refer to chapter 1 for a list of iPad accessories.

Figure 3.8. GarageBand Smart Guitar.

VIDEO 3.4 HANDYSHELL FOR IPAD DEMO.

Figure 3.9. http://vimeo.com/43412590

VIDEO 3.5. GARAGEBAND SMART GUITAR DEMO.

Figure 3.10.
http://youtu.be/H7KjEB_SGf0

Bass

There are bass options that are similar to the guitar options. Choose from a Liverpool, Muted, Picked, or Upright bass; then select chords or notes and jam away.

Strings

GarageBand Strings refers to classical or orchestral strings, as opposed to guitar or bass. Choose from violin, viola, cello, or string bass, and decide if you want to play chords or notes. You can also select more than one string instrument to combine sounds, just as you would in a symphony orchestra.

Figure 3.11. GarageBand Strings.

VIDEO 3.6. GARAGEBAND STRINGS DEMO.

Figure 3.12.
http://youtu.be/hHMf9JJBDq4

ThumbJam

Another all-in-one app like GarageBand is ThumbJam. They both offer similar features. You don't necessarily need both GarageBand and ThumbJam for performance. One or the other would be sufficient.

ThumbJam by Sonosaurus LLC ($8.99)

https://itunes.apple.com/ca/app/thumbjam/id338977566?mt=8

ThumbJam comes with more than 40 real instruments multisampled exclusively for the app. *Multisampled* refers to the way the instruments are recorded so they sound as real as possible. As in GarageBand, you can use dozens of scales to allow you to improvise with almost any song style or genre style, from rock to classical.

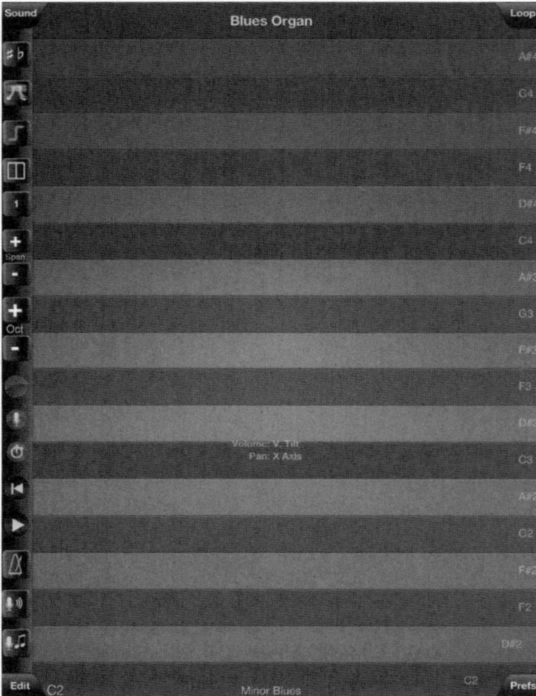

Figure 3.13. ThumbJam: http://thumbjam.com.

The instruments include most of the most common ones, and additional instruments can be downloaded from the app website for free.

- Keyboard: Grand Piano, Drawbar Organ (2 types), Rhodes, Pipe Organ.
- Strings: Cello, Violin, Upright Bass (plucked and bowed).
- Brass: Trumpet, Trombone.
- Woodwinds: Flute, Tenor Sax.
- Guitar, Bass and other Plucked Strings: Electric Guitar, Acoustic Guitar, Electric Bass, Mandolin, Cittern.
- Drums and Percussion: Drum set, Darabukka, Djembe.
- Synths: Synth Strings, Synth Choir, Theremin, Sawtooth Waveform, Sine Waveform, Triangle Waveform, JR Zendrix, JR Smooth Steel.
- Other Instruments: Melodica, Scottish Smallpipes, Hammered Dulcimer.

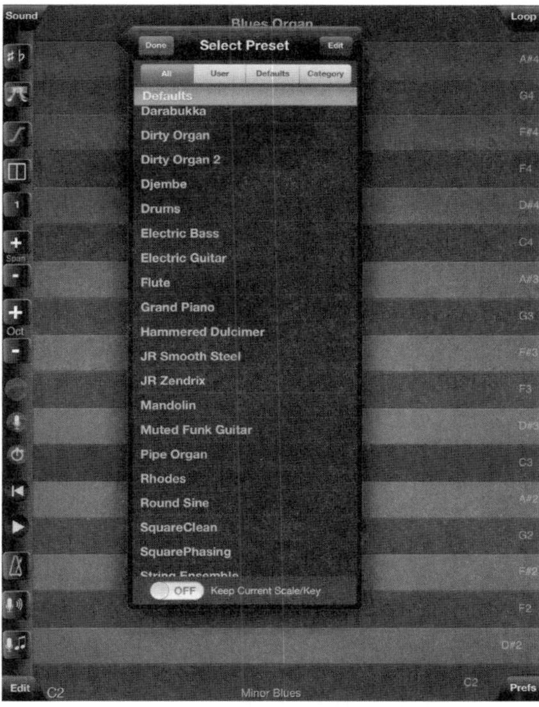

Figure 3.14. ThumbJam Instruments.

The scale settings in ThumbJam blow GarageBand away. ThumbJam has more than 100 different scales grouped into general categories. There are 14 different blues scales and over 40 modal scales alone.

The look and feel of the app is not as sleek as GarageBand, and there is only one way to view the instruments—no virtual keyboard or guitar to tap. This makes it better to use as an improvisation instrument than for playing a specific melody or tune. However, there are many more instrument options for you to choose from. Also, controlling the app is a snap. You can even use vibrato and panning. *Panning* refers to the place of the sound in the left or right speaker. Move your finger side to side for tremolo, up and down for pitch vibrato, and back and forth to change the panning.

VIDEO 3.7. THUMBJAM DEMO.

Figure 3.15.
http://thumbjam.com/media

ThumbJam, like GarageBand, includes the option of looping tracks and recording your improvisations. There will be more on this feature in chapter 5.

All-in-One Summary

GarageBand and ThumbJam are two similar apps. They both offer a variety of instruments to play and the ability to record and loop tracks. If you want the most options for live improvisation, then ThumbJam is the way to go. But GarageBand has features that make it a winner in the live-performance area, especially if you want to play melodies using virtual instruments such as piano, guitar, and drums.

> **Tip:** With apps, since they are either free or relatively inexpensive, you can't download a demo before you purchase. There are a couple of things to do if the app is not free and you're unsure if you would like to download it. First, check the user ratings. Then, go to YouTube or the company website and look for demonstration videos. This will give you an idea of the look and feel of the app before you decide to purchase it.

Individual Instruments and Instrument Families

So, what if GarageBand or ThumbJam or another app that features multiple instruments does not have the instrument you are looking for? There are apps that focus on specific instruments and/or instrument families. Also, since these apps focus on specific instruments, they often include features that enhance live performance.

Keyboards

GarageBand has some excellent keyboard sounds and performance options. However, some other apps offer some attractive enhancements.

Pianist Pro by MooCowMusic Ltd. ($4.99)

https://itunes.apple.com/us/app/pianist-pro/id358857758?mt=8&ign-mpt=uo%3D4

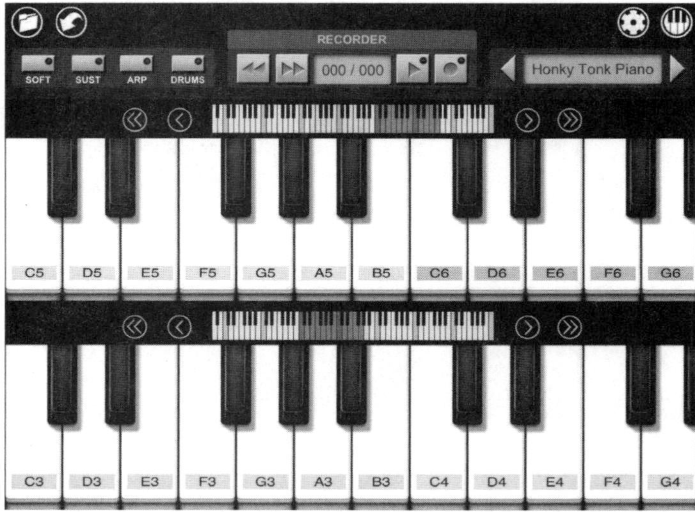

Figure 3.16. Pianist Pro.

If you know how to play the piano even a little bit, this app will be a lot of fun and produce some really pleasing results. The piano sound is excellent, and it includes more than a dozen other keyboard and non-keyboard sounds. Pianist Pro allows you to play one or two keyboards at once and has simple controls to change the octave.

The app has a built-in drum machine that includes many drum patterns that can easily be changed, adjusted, and programmed, which can help you stay in time as you play. You can program your own drum patterns using an easy-to-program drum kit as well.

It also has preset scales, so you can change from the standard piano keyboard to a linear layout (see Fig. 3.10). You can select from common scales such as major, minor, and pentatonic.

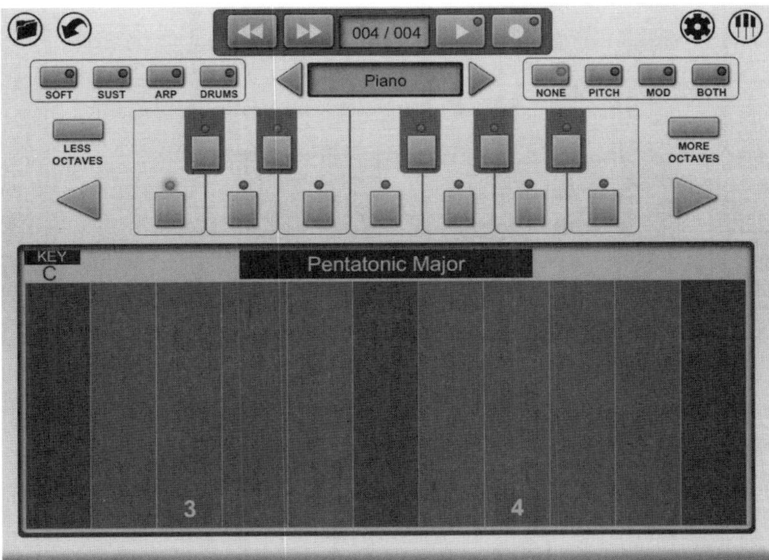

Figure 3.17. Pianist Pro Scale window.

VIDEO 3.8. PIANIST PRO.

Figure 3.18.
http://youtu.be/AKZDNX3rTP8

Organ+ by Yonac Inc. ($2.99)

https://itunes.apple.com/us/app/organ/id420480324?mt=8&ign-mpt=uo%3D4

The cool thing about apps that are dedicated to one instrument is the detail they offer. These apps are able to incorporate details that bring you closer to the experience you might have using the real instrument. In Organ+, draw bars are presented to tweak a sound, just as if you were on a Hammond organ.

It includes seven organ engines that recreate the sounds of transistor and tonewheel organs. The FX stack—with dual chorus/vibrato, vintage-y reverb, overdrive, and more—lets you create ample variation.

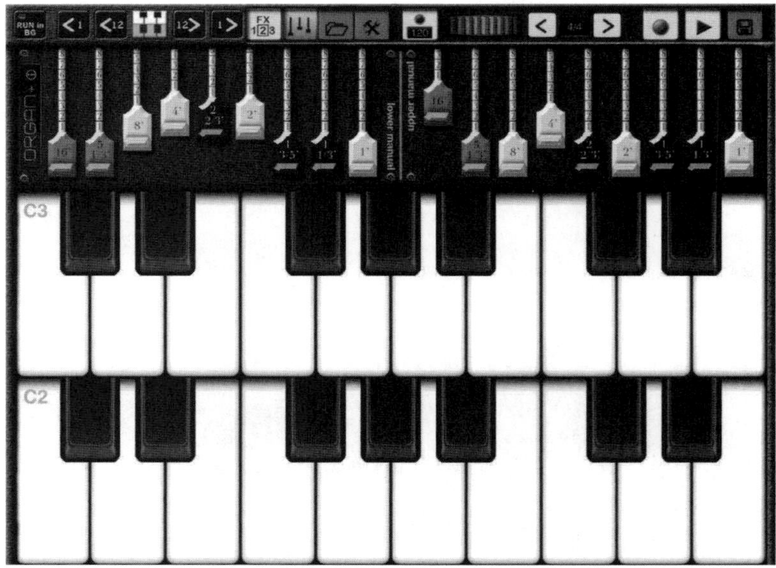

Figure 3.19. Organ+.

Organ+, like Pianist Pro, offers two keyboards or manuals. Both are individually adjustable with nine drawbars each, giving you distinct tones that improve phrasing and effect. You can set organ key clicks and percussion.

VIDEO 3.9. ORGAN+.

Figure 3.20.
www.youtube.com/watch?feature=player_embedded&v=oC-mkYcSF5w

Drums and Percussion

The layout of the drum set in GarageBand is not optimized for playing in live performance. If you are looking for an app to play drums live, then one of the dedicated percussion apps is the way to go.

Rhythm Pad Free (Drums/Drum Pad) by JSplash Apps (Free)

https://itunes.apple.com/sg/app/rhythm-pad-free-drums-drum-pad/id504321020?mt=8

Rhythm Pad (Drums/Drum Pad) by JSplash Apps ($4.99)

https://itunes.apple.com/us/app/rhythm-pad-drums-drum-pad/id457863522?mt=8

Rhythm Pad has both a free option and $4.99 version. The benefit of this app is that the drums are assigned to pads and are easier to play with your hands. There are many kits available, and the free version works essentially the same as the $4.99 version; there are just ads at the bottom of the screen. So if you can tolerate advertisements, you can save a few dollars and get the same app experience.

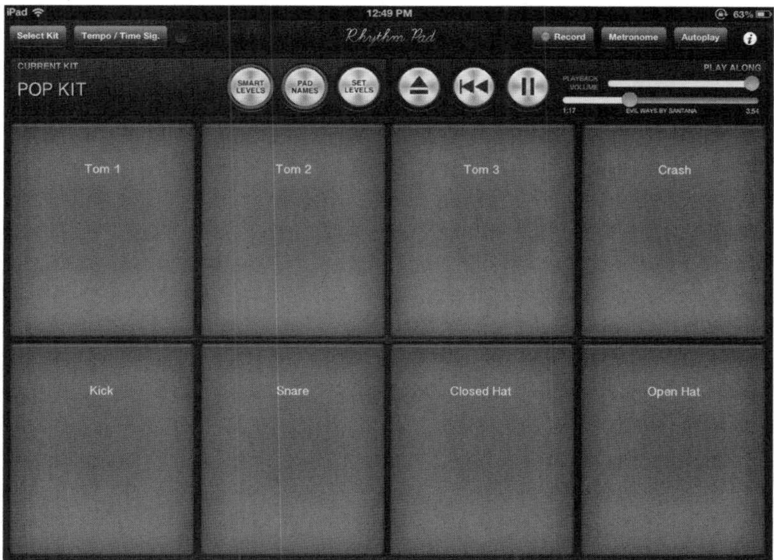

Figure 3.21. Rhythm Pad.

You can select from a variety of drum sets, each with its own appropriate sounds for rock, hip-hop, dance/club, and more. You can record your drum grooves and share them with others. There is also a metronome option to help you keep time.

You can program the pads so they are in the location that is most comfortable to you. There is a built-in option to access your iTunes music library to load songs to play along with, which is great for fun practicing.

VIDEO 3.10. RHYTHM PAD DEMO.

Figure 3.22.
www.youtube.com/watch?v=gVBbgiXt9Ak

Tambourine by Crimson Technology Inc. ($2.99)

https://itunes.apple.com/us/app/tambourine/id400873541?mt=8

This app has several percussion instruments that you dial up one at a time. Included are tambourine, maracas, triangle, guiro, and castanets. You can tap or shake the iPad to play it! There is a free version that only includes the tambourine: https://itunes.apple.com/us/app/tambourine!/id343819796?mt=8.

Guitar

GuitarStudio by Frontier Design Group ($4.99)

https://itunes.apple.com/us/app/guitarstudio/id291921788?mt=8

GuitarStudio is an excellent-sounding guitar app with controls for chords and melody. Played using 6-string, 12-string, or nylon-string sound packs, plucked or picked, GuitarStudio features AirPlay with over 4,000 shared songs from all over the world that you can play along and learn from. No music experience is required. There are shared songs that are easily accessible.

VIDEO 3.11. GUITARSTUDIO DEMO.

Figure 3.23.
www.youtube.com/watch?v=nfJRTgJDxUU&list=PL6E6A1F2F3AD36E04&index=1

Brass

iTrump 2-inch Trumpet with Trumpad by Spoonjack ($2.99)

https://itunes.apple.com/us/app/itrump-2-inch-trumpet-trumpad/id412671325?mt=8

iTrump uses the layout of the iPad well to let you play tunes. You can record performances and play along with tracks. It lays out the chromatic notes in the same way a trumpet plays them, following the overtone or harmonic series: http://en.wikipedia.org/wiki/Harmonic_series_%28music%29. Bugle calls are a snap to play!

iTrump is recommended for beginners. It does not have built-in scales, so you have to know the notes you want to play. It also has a "follow the notes" option, where you play along with songs so you can learn by watching the notes fly by on the screen. If you are familiar with playing trumpet, then you may enjoy this app.

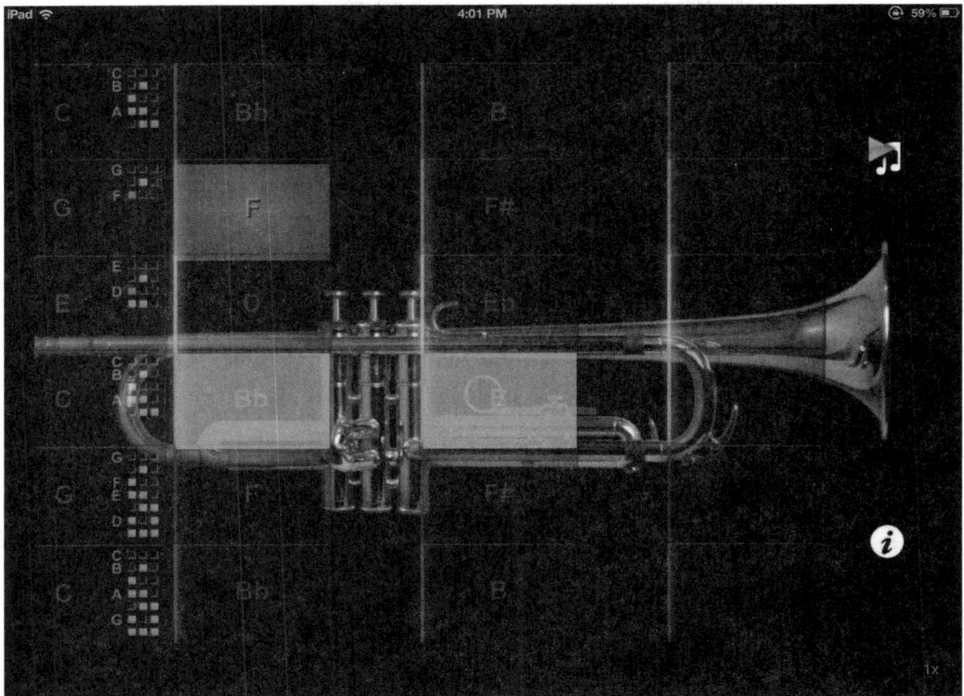

Figure 3.24. iTrump.

VIDEO 3.12. ITRUMP.

Figure 3.25.
www.youtube.com/watch?v=lJrN4z8ZOMY

Trombone

iBone—The Pocket Trombone by Spoonjack ($2.99)

https://itunes.apple.com/us/app/ibone-the-pocket-trombone/id306629300?mt=8

iBone is another app from the same company that produces iTrump that gives you a fun and realistic feel of the trombone.

VIDEO 3.13. IBONE DEMO.

Figure 3.26.
www.youtube.com/watch?v=pw9t-K5GdPs

Woodwinds

There are dedicated apps for woodwinds and saxophones as well.

Saxophone musicofx by mode of expression, LLC ($0.99)

https://itunes.apple.com/us/app/saxophone-musicofx/id309545453?mt=8

This app is designed to emulate the look and feel of the saxophone and is played by touch. Check out the demo. It is designed for the iPhone/iPod Touch but can be used on the iPad as well.

VIDEO 3.14. SAXOPHONE DEMO.

Figure 3.27.
www.youtube.com/watch?v=_o6_J4fDnLY

Tip: When you purchase or download an app, it can also be installed on other iOS devices—for example, your iPhone or iPod Touch.

Nonstandard Instruments

Holiday Bells by Lightsphere LLC ($0.99)

https://itunes.apple.com/us/app/holiday-bells/id300097303?mt=8

This app is two instruments in one. It includes sleigh bells that you can tap or shake, and single handbells that can be tuned like the ones used in many churches. The bell rings when you move the iPad with a fast down or up motion. There is also a keyboard of bells that are aligned in the shape a piano keyboard, which is a lot of fun.

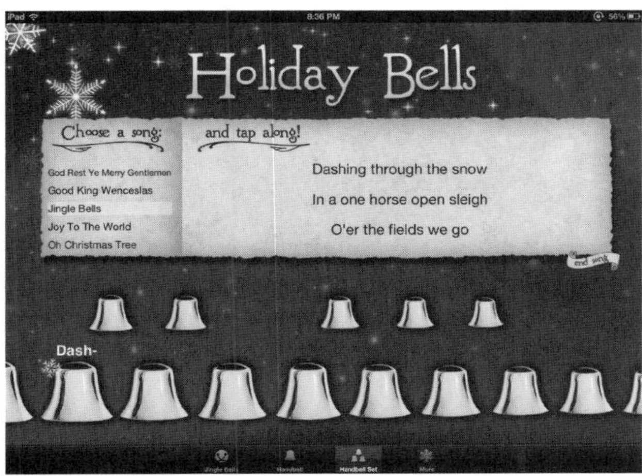

Figure 3.28. Holiday Bells.

It comes with twelve Christmas songs you can tap along to by following the snowflakes. The iPad version includes the lyrics to all the songs! This app can be fun for any age, especially around the Christmas holiday.

> **Tip:** You can play along with any song on your iPad with any of the instrument apps. Go to iTunes and start a song. Then go to the instrument app and play along. Double-tap the Home button and the apps that are running are at the bottom of the screen.

Gestrument by Jesper Nordin ($9.99)

https://itunes.apple.com/us/app/id576235482

This is one of the most innovative app instruments available. Rather than trying to emulate acoustic instruments, this app uses the features of the iPad to create a unique instrument that is fun and can enhance your creativity. You can improvise or compose within the scales and rhythms you choose. Use parameters such as pulse density, scale morphing, rhythm randomness, or pitch fluctuation to find new paths for musical expression and creativity. You can play on up to eight instruments at once—all with different individual settings.

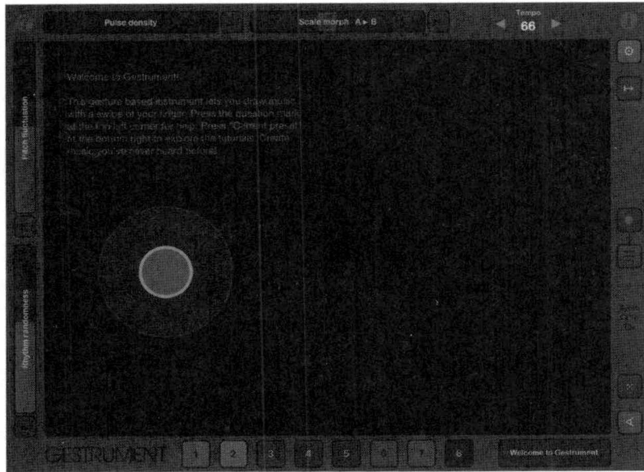

Figure 3.29. Gestrument.

VIDEO 3.15. GESTRUMENT DEMO.

Figure 3.30.
www.youtube.com/watch?v=z8JIlKxqr1o

Theremin

After playing around with several of the theremin apps, ThumbJam, discussed in the "All-in-One" section earlier in this chapter, has a couple of excellent theremin options. The finger controls the pitch, panning and vibrato, and tilting, while the iPad controls the volume.

VIDEO 3.16. THUMBJAM THEREMIN DEMO.

Figure 3.31.
http://youtu.be/Y47zP_-QNf8

Electronic Instruments

Over the years, there have been many shapes and sizes of synthesizers. In the past, to be a serious keyboard player usually involved lugging around at least two or more keyboards. The recent trend in developing instruments with software allows the modern keyboardist to use controller keyboards, which are significantly lighter, to control virtual synthesizers on a laptop computer. The iPad is entering the synthesizer arena with some familiar names—and plenty of new ones.

> **Tip:** To use any iPad app with a USB MIDI keyboard, make sure that the app supports Core MIDI. Plug the USB cable from the keyboard into the iPad Camera Connector (sold separately).

There are many synthesizer apps found in the App Store. Some are free downloads, allowing you to download and sample the patches and interfaces so you can choose favorites and delete the rest. Paid synthesizer apps can cost anywhere from $0.99 to $49.99, still well beneath the average cost of most computer soft synths.

When you are looking through the specs of musical instrument apps in the App Store, there are a few terms you'll see in the descriptions for apps. If a specific function is important to you, then be sure to look for it before you purchase.

Terms for Synthesizer Apps

- AudioCopy/AudioPaste: Developed by Sonoma Wire Works, AudioCopy allows supporting apps to copy an audio clip, generated by the app, to a pasteboard where it can be pasted into another app supporting AudioPaste. You will be able to review your audio clip both after copying and before pasting into the destination app. Sonoma Wire Works supports a developer program for app developers who wish to incorporate the technology into their apps. A list of supported apps can be found at www.sonomawireworks.com/iphone/audiocopy/.
- Audio Recording Function: This function enables an app to record its own audio output to the iPad as an audio file. This file can be sent out directly to a cloud site or social media site, or via e-mail.
- Audiobus: Audiobus is an app that facilitates communication between apps, allowing you to link multiple apps together for layering, processing, and recording. For a list of supported apps, check the company's website at www.audiob.us.
- Background Audio: Background Audio allows an app to continue playing audio even when it is in the background of the iOS's multitasking environment. This allows iTunes to keep playing while you check e-mail or surf the web. A synth supporting Background Audio will be able to continue playing when sent to the background when you launch another app.
- Core MIDI: Core MIDI support allows an app to be triggered by an external MIDI device, most commonly a MIDI keyboard, but all MIDI controllers, such as percussion pads or wind controllers, will work with a Core MIDI app.
- Kaoss Pad: Korg's Kaoss Pad controller has been around since 1999. It is part effects device, with its own internal suite of effects, part sampler, and part MIDI controller. The Kaoss Pad uses the X–Y axis controller of the original hardware device to alter the sound of a synth patch in real time.
- Sampler: An app with sampling capability can record sound using either the internal mic on the iPad or a mic attached with an adapter, such as a USB mic that is attached using the Apple Camera Adapter. You can then use that sound in performance.
- Sequencer: The sequencer found in most apps is not something as powerful as the computer or keyboard DAWs on the market today; it is usually a 16-step sequencer similar to the old analog sequencers from the '70s.
- Tabletop: Tabletop is an app that creates a virtual studio environment in the iPad where multiple apps can work together to create a track. Tabletop is a free app, but has its own suite of instruments that are available in app purchases. For a list of supported apps, check the company's website: http://retronyms.com.
- USB: The most common USB adapter is Apple's Camera Adapter, which plugs into the 30-pin or Lightning port of the iPad. Any USB MIDI keyboard can be plugged into the Camera Adapter to control an iOS synth. There are several other adapters, such as IK Multimedia's iRig MIDI, that have MIDI In, Out, and Thru ports for integration into a larger MIDI setup.
- Virtual MIDI Input Port: An app supporting Virtual MIDI Input can receive MIDI data from another app running on the same IOS device. This allows you to layer sounds from multiple devices or use one as a controller for another.
- WIST: Wireless Sync-Start Technology is an open-source technology developed by Korg and is available for free to all app developers. This allows two iPads, using WIST, to run in sync using Bluetooth.

Retro Synths

iMini by Arturia ($9.99)

www.arturia.com/evolution/en/products/iMini/intro.html

Some of the most popular software instruments are recreations of older analog synthesizers. The classic Mini Moog, known for both bass sounds and leads, is a must-have in any synth collection. Arturia, having already produced the minimoog V2 soft synth, brings Mini Moog sound to the iPad as the iMini. All of the front-panel knobs and switches are active and allow live modification of the sound.

Figure 3.32.

> **Tip:** If you already own the minimoog V2 soft synth, any presets you own or have created are fully compatible with the iMini. You can import patches to or export them from your iPad by using the 30-pin or Lightning cable connector cable connector to connect your iPad with the computer. You can manage the patches in iTunes.

iMini has two additional control panel views in addition to the Main page. They can be selected with the red buttons at the top of the screen. The Perform panel contains an arpeggiator and two XY controller "joystick" pads. Each can be assigned to a different synth parameter for use during recording or performance. The strip between the panel and the keyboard contains the keyboard controls that govern the octave, portamento, decay, and legato, and the scale or key.

Figure 3.33.

The third panel is the FX panel. There are two simple effects: Chorus and Analog Delay. Along the top of the screen is the Connect panel that handles communication between iMini and other apps or external MIDI devices.

Figure 3.34.

iMini supports two new and important features that expand the iPad's capabilities. The first is called WIST, an acronym for Wireless Sync-Start Technology, which was developed by Korg. This allows you to sync two iPads, running WIST apps, using Bluetooth. The second is Tabletop, which is a separate free app that allows supported apps to be incorporated into a virtual studio environment with other Tabletop apps. In the Tabletop app, you can run multiple versions of supported apps, automate features of synths, and purchase additional apps by Retronyms, the developer of Tabletop.

Tip: Korg, the developer of WIST, keeps a list of WIST-supported apps at www.korguser.net/wist/.

VIDEO 3.17. IMINI.

Figure 3.35.
http://youtu.be/-aoIKCS_jsY

iMS20 by Korg ($29.99)

www.korg.com/ims20

For those of you who remember patch chords, the Korg iMS 20 will give you the opportunity to patch modules together, virtually, in a recreation of the Korg MS 20 analog synthesizer. In addition to the functioning knobs, the signal can be routed using virtual patch cords. Just tap the output port and drag your finger to an input port to connect them.

Figure 3.36. Korg iMS20.

The app adds a 6-voice, 16-step drum sequencer that can be programmed using virtual switches or played in using virtual pad controllers along the bottom of the screen. You can have up to 16 patterns in the app's memory.

Figure 3.37.

The audio for each of the 6 voices can be mixed using an onboard mixer. A single effect can be applied to the drum mix, but you can select specific tracks for the effect to be applied to, should you not want it applied to all voices. Another retro feature is the Analog 16-Step Sequencer. It is possible to create complete compositions in the iMS 20. Saved files can be offloaded via iTunes or uploaded to SoundCloud directly from the app.

Figure 3.38.

VIDEO 3.18. KORG IMS20.

Figure 3.39.
www.korg.com/iPad_Apps

Korg iPolysix by Korg ($29.99)

www.korg.com/iPolysix

Korg has converted their popular '80s-era Polysix keyboard into an app as well. The features are similar to the iMS 20, with drum sequencer and pattern sequencer features to allow complete song production within the app. Users can upload tracks to Polyshare, a SoundCloud-like site for iPolysix users to share music and connect. A video introduction is available at the Korg web link listed above, or follow the link in Figure 3.39.

Figure 3.40.

iElectribe by Korg ($19.99)

www.korg.com/ielectribe

Modern dance music can trace its roots back to the '70s and the first drum machines. The sounds of those early machines are still staples in dance and electronic music. Recreating those classic beat boxes in the iPad is easy, as their memory requirements are low, and they are particularly suited to the iOS world of hands-on interface. Korg offers an iOS version of the Electribe drum machine, the iElectribe. The iElectribe has a large library of patterns that can be used or modified and saved. Each pattern can have eight parts: four analog-modeled synthesizer parts and four PCM waveform parameters for open and closed hi-hat, cymbal, hand-clap, and snare. The iElectribe has WIST technology built in so it can be used with any other WIST-capable app on another iPad. A video introduction is available at the Korg web link listed above, or follow the link in Figure 3.39.

Figure 3.41.

iMPC by Akai ($6.99)

www.akaiprompc.com/impc

Akai's MPC has been reproduced, to some degree, as the iMPC, allowing you to physically perform your percussion track by tapping the pads on the screen. In addition to the internal sounds, there is a sampling option, allowing you to create your own drum kits and effects. There is a four-track mixer screen and effects screen to further enhance the sound. The iMPC is WIST capable, so it can be synced with other WIST apps on other iPads, and it also supports Tabletop, allowing it to be used with other Tabletop apps on the same iPad.

Figure 3.42.

For easier handling in live performance, Akai offers MPC Fly 30, a laptop-like case with control buttons, performance pads, and transport controls taking the place of the keyboard, and a dock to hold the iPad in the screen position.

VIDEO 3.19. AKAI IMPC DEMO.

Figure 3.43.
http://www.youtube.com/watch?v=QDAwVNz3aXs

ReBirth for iPad by Reason ($14.99)

www.rebirthapp.com/

From the computer world, there is a rebirth of ReBirth. From the folks who bring you Reason, ReBirth brings back the sounds of Roland's 303 Bass synth; the app actually has two of them, allowing for more complex parts, and the TR 808 and 909 drum machines. There is an effects section and a mixer for enhancing the sonic pallet. ReBirth can be synced with any WIST app on another iPad or work with an Audiobus app in the same iPad. A video introduction is available at the rebirth web link listed above.

Figure 3.44.

DXi FM by Takashi Mizuhiki ($1.99)

www.taktech.org/takm/DXie/DXi_for_iPhone.html

Retro now includes digital synths. FM synthesis dominated the decade of the '80s and is represented on the iPad by the DXi FM synthesizer by Takashi Mizuhiki. It is a 4-operator FM synth, similar to the Yamaha TX81z, with a 16-step loop sequencer added. It has 69 preset sounds and 29 blank preset spaces to create your own sounds. Select from 8 sine-wave variations—square, saw triangle waves, or white noise to begin—or edit an already existing sound. The effects section is a nice touch to add some additional character and expressiveness to the sounds. A video introduction is available at the web link listed above.

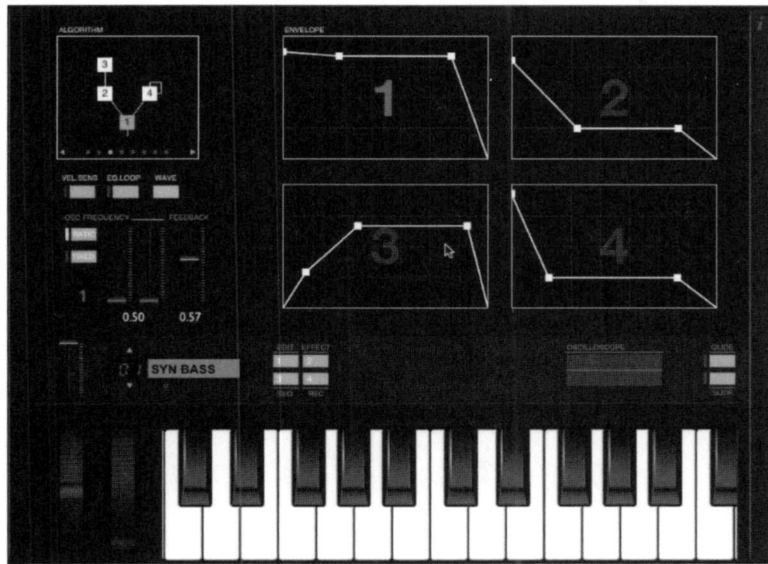

Figure 3.45.

Peter Vogel CMI by Peter Vogel Instruments Pty Ltd (Base Version $9.99, Pro Version $49.99)

www.fairlightinstruments.com.au/ios/

One of the most coveted synths of its day was the Fairlight CMI (computer music instrument). The Fairlight CMI was featured on many pop records in the '80s, as well as heard regularly on TV on the *Miami Vice* soundtrack. Due to the $50,000–$100,000 price tag, most people bought a DX7 or Roland D50 and wished for a hit record. Fairlight developer Peter Vogel has brought the Fairlight experience to the iPad as the Peter Vogel CMI app, complete with floppy-disk loading sounds. This app is available in two forms, a base version that sells for $9.99 and a Pro version that sells for $49.99 (a hefty price in the world of apps, but even with the purchase price of the iPad thrown in, now less expensive than a new DX7). The base version of the app has the classic 8-bit CMI X II samples and the ability to load and play songs in the Page R eight-track sequencer.

Figure 3.46.

The Pro version allows you access to the 16-bit CMI III library of sounds and the ability to sample and save sounds, create and edit your own instrument sets and songs, and import and export Fairlight voice files.

VIDEO 3.20. PETER VOGEL CMI DIGITAL SYNTHS.

Figure 3.47.
http://petervogelinstruments.com.au/ios/video-tutorial-part-1/

iLectric Piano by IK Multimedia ($9.99)

www.ikmultimedia.com/products/ilectricipad/

Though not truly synths, the electric piano and organ are staples of the pop keyboard sound. Both are well represented in GarageBand, but for those going a different route, there are other options. iLectric from IK Multimedia provides a 20-preset menu of variations on the electric piano, with an additional 20 available via an in-app purchase. Sounds include variations of classic Rhodes models as well as the Wurlitzer electric piano. IK Multimedia also markets iGrand Piano, a similar app with acoustic pianos. There is a free version with a single grand piano, and a bonus piano if you register the app online.

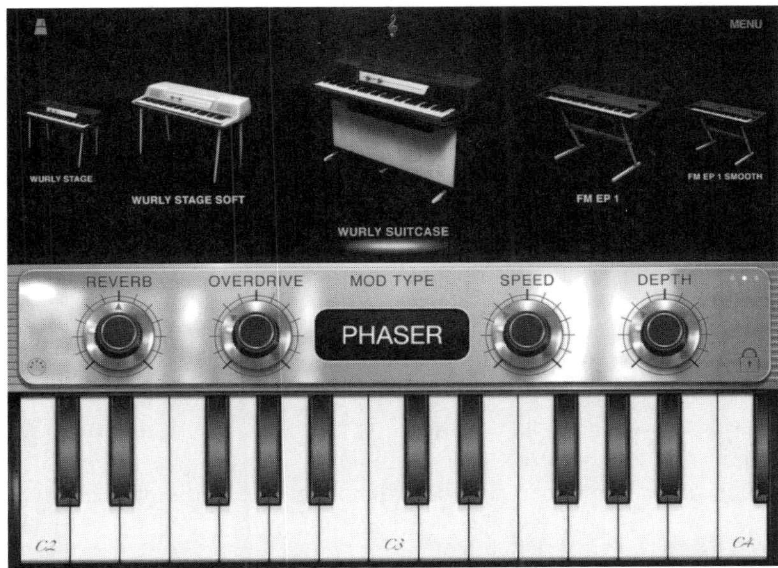

Figure 3.48.

Mellotronics M3000 for iPad by Omenie ($11.99)

www.omenie.com/M3000%20refresh/M3000_refresh/M3000_HD.html

Another non-synth but classic retro keyboard is the Mellotron. The original device triggered tape loops to produce sound. The creators of the original Mellotron have joined forces with Omenie Software and digitized the original tapes to create the Mellotronics M3000 for iPad. The app supports four voices being played at once but is currently without Core MIDI support, so performance is only possible using the onscreen keyboard.

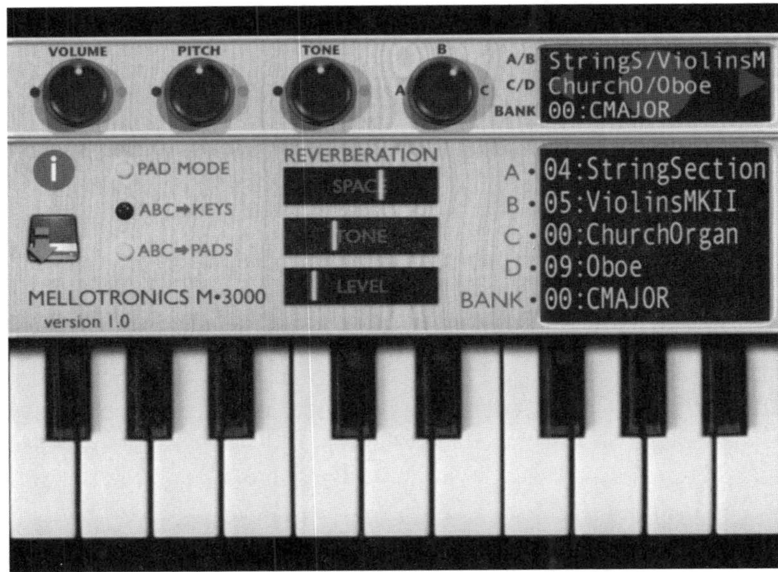

Figure 3.49.

Contemporary Synth Apps

The world of new synth apps on the iPad can be divided into two categories: apps that use a standard keyboard controller or tap pad (for percussion) interfaces, and apps that try and take advantage of the hands-on nature of the iOS interface to create alternate approaches to triggering and manipulating sound.

Traditional Interfaces

NLogSynth PRO by Tempo Rubato ($9.99)

www.temporubato.com/

The NLogSynth PRO app from Tempo Rubato is a great example of a traditional synthesizer interface done well as an iOS device. Originally an iPhone app, the iPad version expands the instrument's control surface so there's more on the screen. The sound is virtual analog, and with support for Core MIDI, WIST, and Audiobus, it plays well with other music apps. A video introduction is available at the web link listed above.

Figure 3.50.

Alchemy by Camel Audio (Free/Pro Upgrade: $14.99/In-App Purchases Available)

www.camelaudio.com/AlchemyMobile.php

Alchemy is a synth app that is based on a traditional keyboard interface for triggering sound, but also has three control areas on the screen for real-time alteration to the sound. Thanks to the multitouch iOS interface, it is possible to use all the control areas simultaneously. A basic sound set is included with the app, which is free, and there are in-app purchases of additional sound sets. A video introduction is available at the web link listed above.

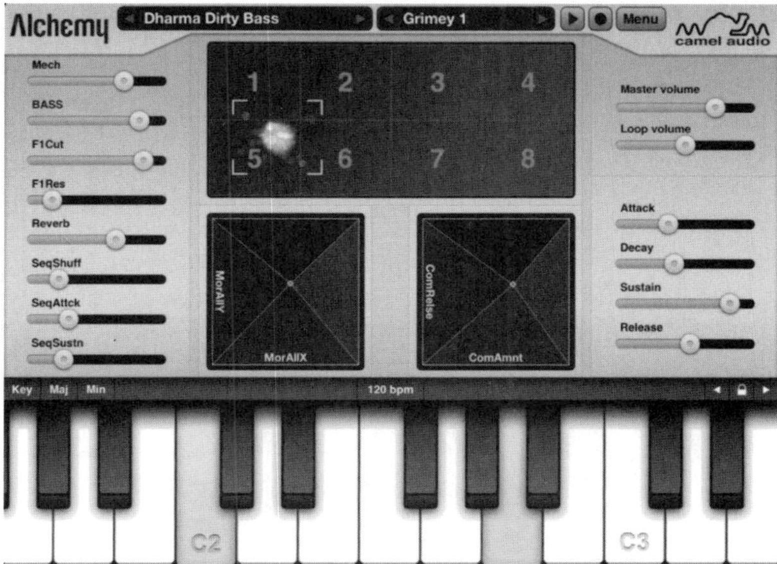

Figure 3.51.

Animoog by Moog Music Inc. ($9.99)

http://moogmusic.com/products/apps/animoog-0#demos-tab

Any app with the name Moog is bound to attract attention and raise expectations. Animoog has a lot of traditional elements but begins the transition to a different interface. It has keys, but not traditional piano-type keys. The range of keys visible on the screen can be adjusted, and the notes available can be adjusted both in range and by pitch. The user can select a specific scale or mode and the root note, then display only the notes in that scale. No wrong notes! A video introduction is available at the web link listed above.

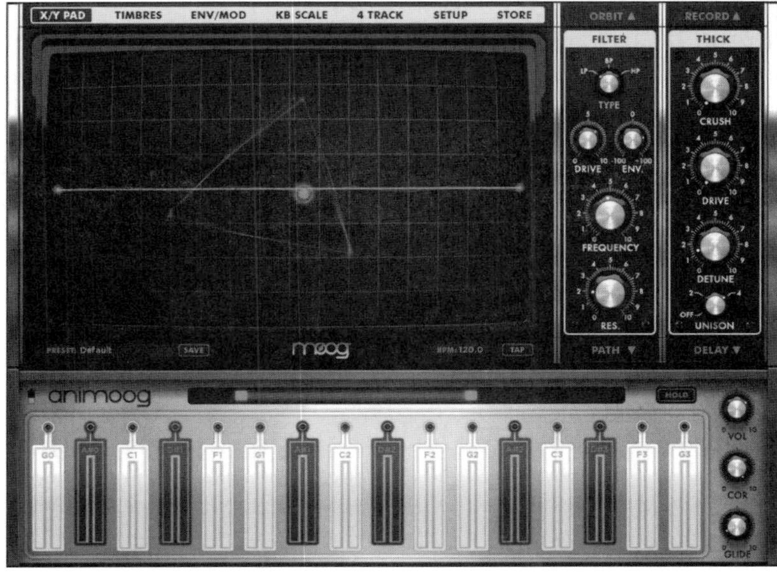

Figure 3.52.

WaveGenerator by Wolfgang Palm (Free/Full Version: $19.95)

https://itunes.apple.com/us/app/wavegenerator/id554998576?mt=8

Another coveted synthesizer name from the '80s is PPG. PPG brings wavetable synthesis to the iOS world. The free app has full access to the sound library but is "feature limited" in the number of voices and other capabilities of the program. One feature that is available is turning a photograph into sound. As with Animoog, the PPG WaveGenerator has a nontraditional keyboard for performance. The sound's timber can be altered by dragging your finger over the keys in different directions. Digging into wavetable synthesis is not for everyone, but this app offers those willing to accept the challenge the chance to be rewarded with some truly unique synth sounds.

Figure 3.53.

DM1 — The Drum Machine by Fingerlab ($4.99)

https://itunes.apple.com/us/app/dm1-the-drum-machine/id431573951?mt=8

It's hard to think of a drum machine app as new, because the classic drum machine sound is retro, but the DM1 is a new app with old sounds, the choice of a 16-step sequencer or tap pads, a mixer to fine-tune the overall mix of your pattern, and just to make it new, an FX page with two X–Y pads to add some real-time effects variations to the sounds.

Figure 3.54.

VIDEO 3.21. DM1 THE DRUM MACHINE FOR IPAD.

Figure 3.55.
http://youtu.be/p-RMgvzCb_8

FunkBox by Synthetic Bits, LLC ($5.99)

http://syntheticbits.com/funkbox.html

If making beats is your main gig, check out FunkBox. What sets this apart from other drum machine apps is the number of different hardware machines represented: fourteen different machines, including the popular Roland, Oberheim, Emulator, and Sequential Circuits models. Funkbox allows you to create custom kits by combining or retuning sounds, or editing the samples themselves.

Figure 3.56.

Figure 3.57.

VIDEO 3.22. FUNKBOX.

Figure 3.58.
http://syntheticbits.com/videos.html

Alternate Interfaces

The iPad's touch screen interface has inspired some app developers to explore how it can free a performer from the traditional piano-key trigger for electronic and sampled sound. These apps can bring an "outside the box" factor to a track, either as a sound source or as a controller for another sound source.

Bebot by Normalware ($1.99)

www.normalware.com/

Bebot is the singing and smiling face many know by now. This app illustrates the approach used by several apps using a non-keyboard interface to trigger sound. Pitch is controlled on the horizontal axis and laid out in increments so you can move up and down in pitch by tapping, or dragging for a legato or portamento effect. As with Animoog, there is the option to select a scale or a mode and root tone, so the instrument will be configured to the desired tonality and only that tonality. Moving vertically on the screen affects the timbre of the sound. One analogy is to think of this type of interface as a flat theremin. A video introduction is available at the web link listed above.

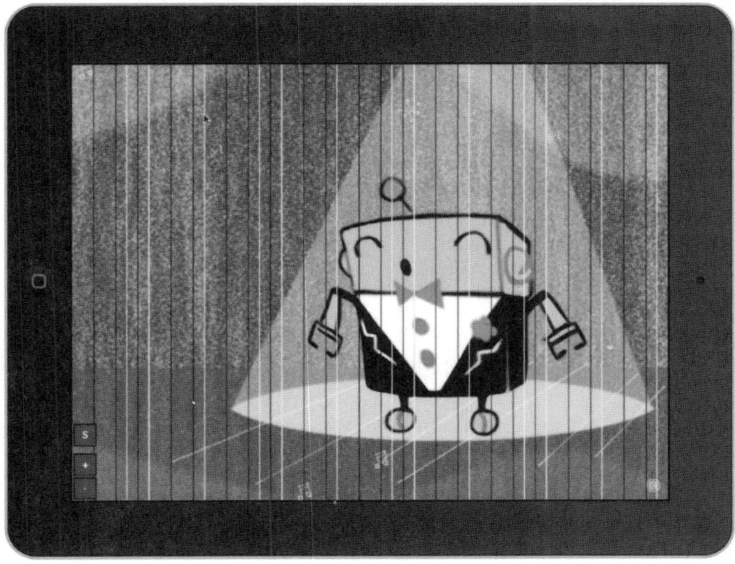

Figure 3.59.

MorphWiz by Wisdom Music, LLC ($9.99)

www.wizdommusic.com/products/morphwiz_tutorial.html

One source of new approaches to music making using iOS devices is Jordan Rudess. MorpWiz uses a vertical-grid approach to sound creation and control similar to Bebot but takes it to a whole new level. This makes it possible to morph between two different sound waves, for example sine and square, in the same patch. It can also do this independently, for 10 voices if you choose to use all available digits. There is a lot of depth beyond the presets.

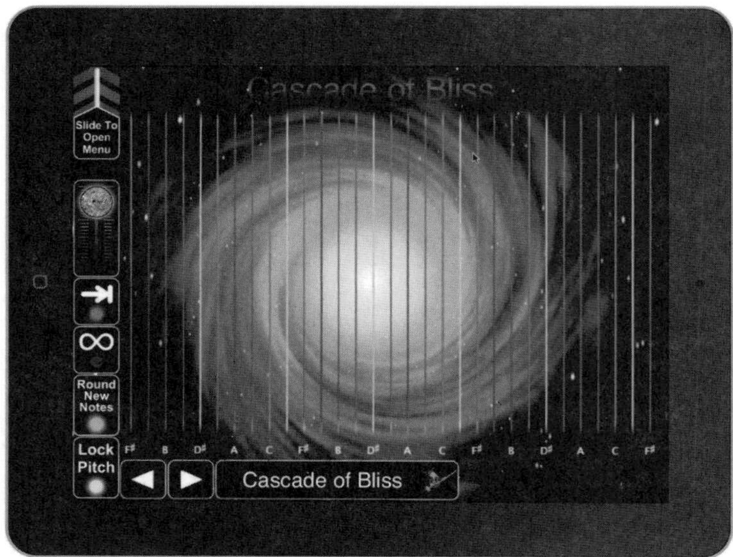

Figure 3.60.

Geo by Wisdom Music, LLC ($9.99)

http://www.wizdommusic.com/products/geo_synthesizer.html

Geo is a synth app with a unique controller interface. It was codeveloped by Rob Fielding and Jordan Rudess. The interface is guitar based with pads arranged in multiple rows ascending in fourths up to the top of the screen. This interface is about note accuracy and, with some practice, being able to play complex guitar or keyboard parts with ease. If you like this interface, codeveloper Rob Fielding has two other apps based on this approach: Mugician is the predecessor and Cantor is the successor to Geo. Geo can be used as a controller app for other iOS apps and can have its sound layered with another app that supports background audio. It can also be used as a controller for any other external MIDI sound source.

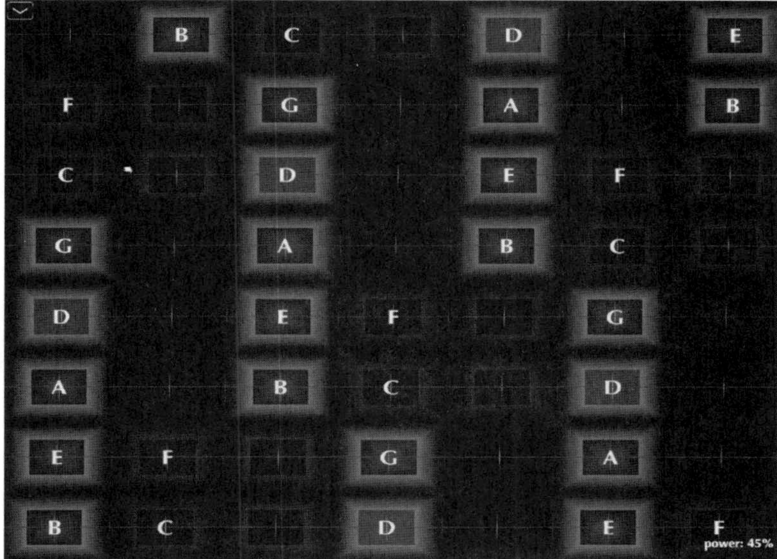

Figure 3.61.

VIDEO 3.23. GEO.

Figure 3.62.
http://youtu.be/-9p_XLanjVE

Sound Prism by Andanika GmbH
(Free/Pro Upgrade: $4.99/In-App Purchases Available)

www.soundprism.com/index_pro.php

Sound Prism is based on a grid interface designed to produce rich harmonic textures. The screen is divided into two sections; on the left is the bass note section with arrows to raise or lower the note by a half step. On the right side is treble grid where you can select one, two, or three notes to sound at a time. There is also an option to have the notes sound in one, two or three different octaves, forming lush chords. There is light and dark shading to the note grid to indicate major chord notes (light) and minor chord notes (darker). The program can be set to a specific key and the notes displayed on screen for easier reference. The iPad's accelerometer can be used to alter the timbre of the sound. It can record its own audio output, and it outputs MIDI, so it can control internal or external synths, or have the MIDI data recorded to another DAW.

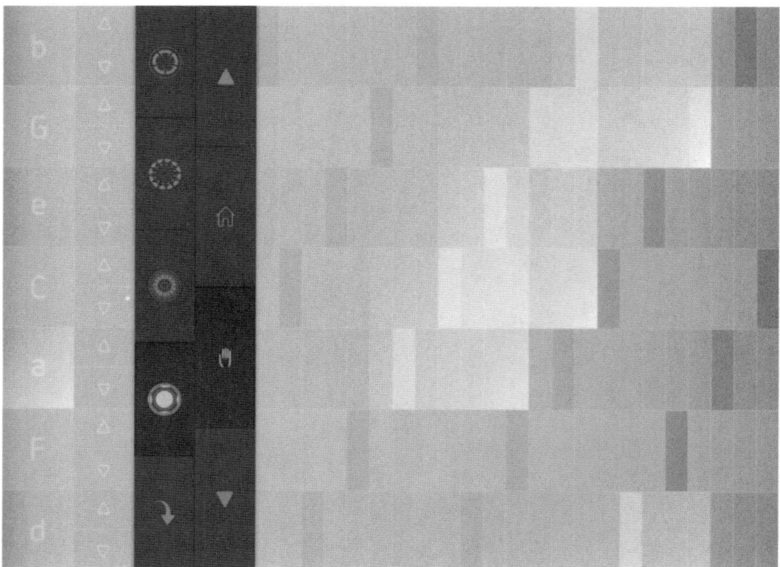

Figure 3.63.

VIDEO 3.24. SOUNDPRISM PRO.

Figure 3.64.
http://youtu.be/d_e8dF5f6Qs

Samplers Old and New

SampleTank by IK Multimedia (Free/Full Version: $5.99/In-App Purchases Available)

www.ikmultimedia.com/products/cat-view.php?C=family-sampletankios

IK Multimedia's SampleTank is a traditional keyboard-based sampler. Sounds are available for most popular acoustic and electric instruments. For many acoustic instruments, SampleTank is the only option for quality sounds in an app that supports Audiobus, and it can be used for recording to apps such as GarageBand, Cubasis and Auria. There is a large library of melodic loops and rhythmic grooves in the app to facilitate loop creation. You can download the free version of the app and add only the sounds you'll need, or purchase the full version and receive a library of sounds across all instrument families, including ethnic instruments and sound EFX. Additional sounds can be purchased in-app. Anyone familiar with sample players on the computer is aware of the disk space all those samples consume. SampleTank is one of the largest apps I've encountered at 805 MB, so make sure you have a lot of free space on your iPad.

Figure 3.65.

SampleWiz by Wisdom Music, LLC ($9.99)

http://www.wizdommusic.com/products/samplewiz.html

SampleWiz is another Jorden Rudess creation that covers the basics of a sampler and then takes them to a level only a touch-screen interface can reach. The app loads in Classic mode with a piano keyboard interface that you can play by tapping on the keys, but you are also able to slide your finger for a portamento effect. This program has the ability to play on the sample wave itself to produce some effects previously only heard when scrubbing an audio file in an editing program. Creating and saving your own samples is easy, as is exporting them to Geo.

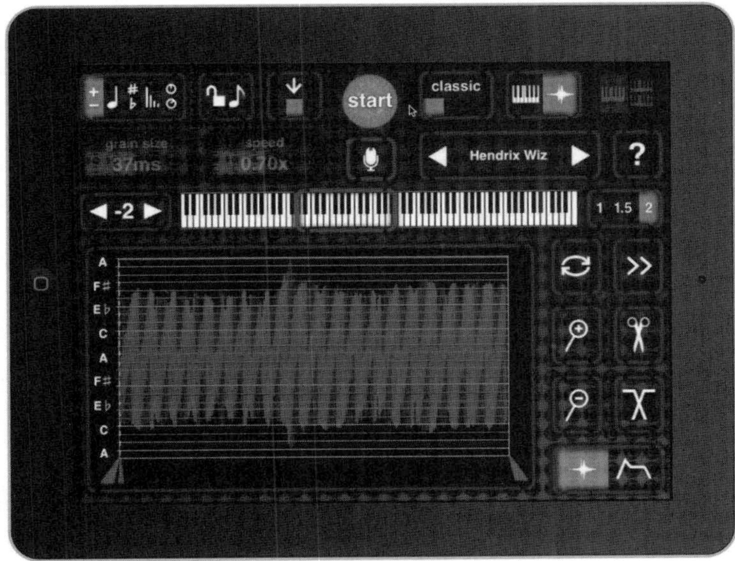

Figure 3.66.

VIDEO 3.25. SAMPLEWIZ.

Figure 3.67.
http://www.wizdommusic.com/products/samplewiz.html

Making Connections

Just as with Mac and Windows computers, musicians can connect devices to the iPad, such as a piano MIDI keyboard. In order to do this, you will need to purchase the Apple iPad Camera Connection Kit.

Connecting a MIDI Keyboard

Apple iPad Camera Connection Kit by Apple Inc. ($29.99)

http://store.apple.com/us/product/MC531ZM/A/apple-ipad-camera-connection-kit?fnode=3a

Any USB MIDI keyboard can be connected to an iPad using the Apple Camera Connector. Plug the Camera Connector into the 30-pin or Lightning port, then plug the USB cable into the Camera Connector. Load any Core MIDI–compliant app, and you are ready to make music. There are Camera Adapter kits available for both 30-pin and Lightening port iPads. Make sure you purchase the correct kit for your device.

Figure 3.68. Apple Camera Connector.

VIDEO 3.26. CONNECTING MIDI.

Figure 3.69.
http://youtu.be/xZOdtZ92iwQ

Audiobus by A Tasty Pixel ($8.99)

http://audiob.us/apps/

Software developers dream of creating the killer app, the one everyone wants to buy, and Audiobus may be that app for iOS musicians. It doesn't make a sound or record a note—or do anything remotely musical—but it will make a lot of music possible. Audiobus serves as the connector between the output of one app and the input of another. There is also the option of routing the audio through a third, effects, app for sound processing. All apps must support Audiobus, so look for Audiobus support in the app's description before you purchase. A list of supported apps is available at the web link above.

Audiobus has three boxes: Input, Effects, and Output. Tap on any box, and a list of supporting apps pops up; select the desired app; then tap again to launch the app and be transferred to it for further setup. Load one app, and a plus sign is added above the Input box, indicating that you can layer input sounds, either with two apps or with a vocal input.

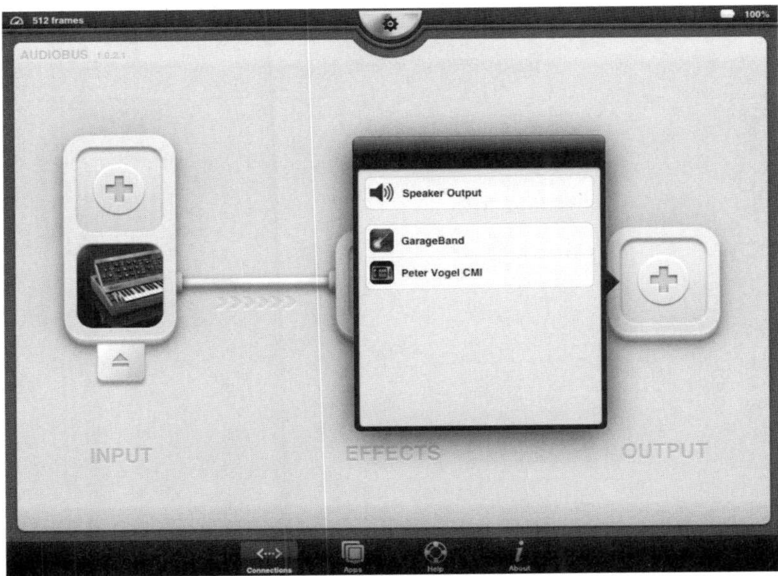

Figure 3.70. Audiobus.

A control panel is placed on the right side of the screen; tap an icon to move between apps. To avoid accidental quitting, Audiobus has a unique shutdown procedure: double-tap the Home button and a row of icons will appear along the bottom of the screen. Scroll to the Audiobus icon, and hold your finger on it until the app icons shake; then tap the red dot with the white dash in the upper-left corner of the icon.

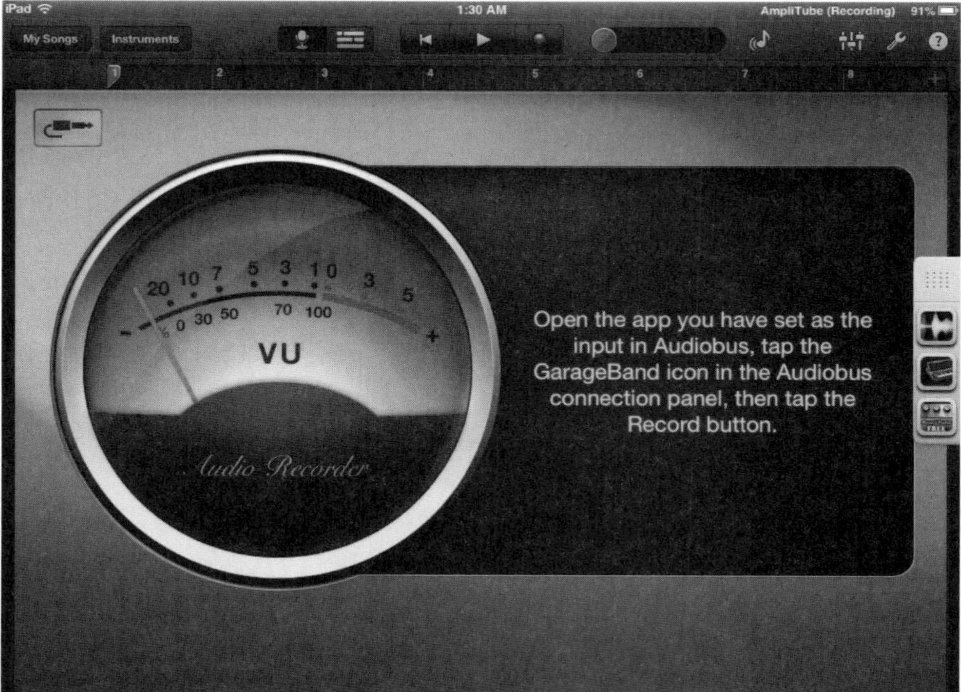

Figure 3.71.

VIDEO 3.27. AUDIOBUS.

Figure 3.72.
http://youtu.be/map8L38ErPI

iConnectMIDI1 by IIConnectivity ($79)

www.iconnectivity.com/iConnectMIDI[1]

iConnectMIDI[1] is a single-input MIDI interface that works with the iPad or computer. It affords the opportunity to connect either a USB or non-USB MIDI keyboard sound module or drum machine.

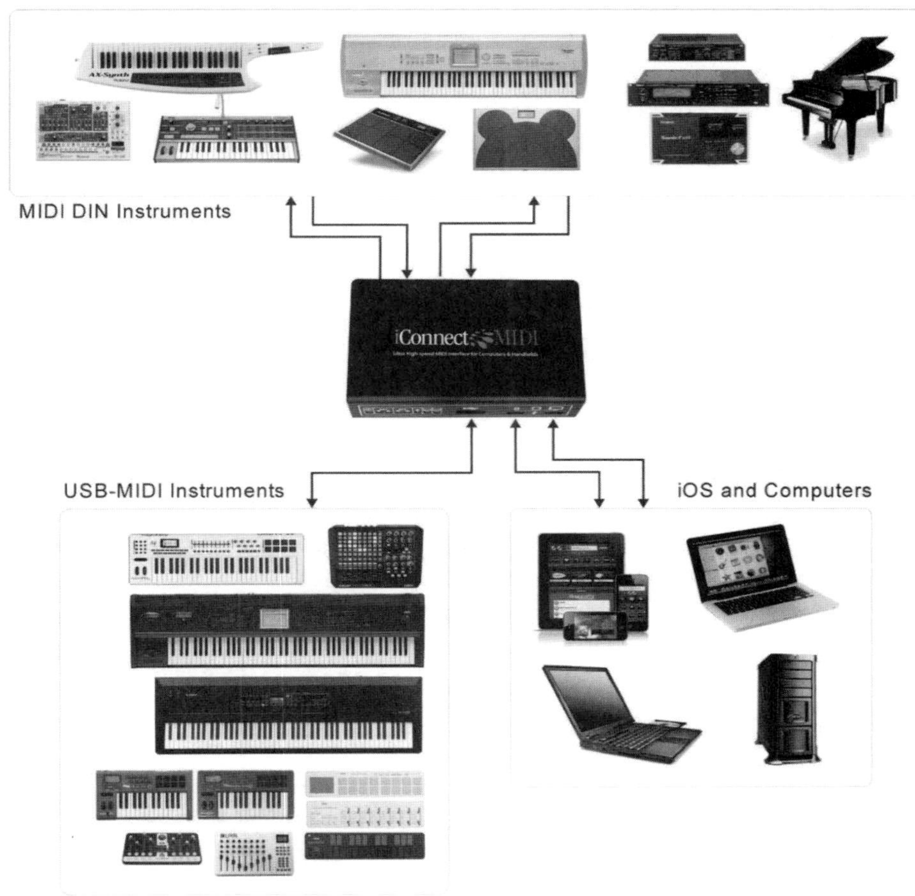

Figure 3.73. iConnectMIDI1.

VIDEO 3.28. iCONNECTMIDI.

Figure 3.74.
http://www.youtube.com/watch?v=_Hk-ETCrzns&feature=share&list=UUcDKN3HsKhjKOCBcxxIP4Gw

Chapter 3 Activities

1. Start playing a song in iTunes or your favorite music service, and then open an app such as GarageBand and play along with the tune.
   a. Click the Record button to record your improvisation.
2. Get together with another iPad user, and jam together on the blues or another chord progression.
3. Perform a round with other performers.
4. Improvise a percussion groove with a tune in iTunes.
5. Connect a MIDI keyboard to your iPad using the Apple iPad Camera Connection Kit.
6. Launch Audiobus and route a synthesizer to GarageBand.

Summary

This chapter focused on using the iPad as a musical instrument to emulate acoustic instruments and create new sounds and instruments specific to the iPad interface. The many options for creating synthesized sounds was also discussed. Connecting other music devices to your iPad is made possible via the Apple iPad Camera Connection Kit. And you can integrate two apps using Audiobus. You should be ready to take your iPad live with one or more of these performance apps.

Chapter 4
Reading Music, Chords, and Lyrics

This chapter will deal with ways to use your iPad to view sheet music, lyrics, and any other type of documents. If you are a performing musician, student, teacher, or music hobbyist, you can have a copy of your music, lyrics, and other documents on your iPad for viewing, practice, and live performance. This can be an indispensable aid when practicing and performing music in any medium, and it can work with almost any instrument or the voice. This chapter will also address what you'll need for hands-free page turning, as well as the various options for connecting your iPad to a stand.

This chapter is organized into the following areas:

1. Viewing music for practice and performance:
   a. Convert music files to PDF format.
   b. Organize the PDF files using a music reader app.
2. Viewing and playing music on your iPad:
   a. Consider using an app for notation files generated by Finale or Sibelius computer-based software.
3. Using an iPad stand and optional hands-free page turner.

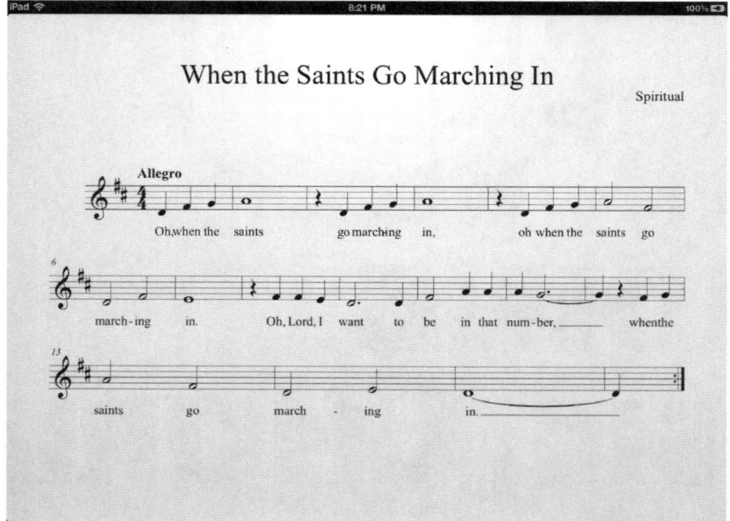

Figure 4.1.

If you are primarily interested in viewing your files so you can reference them as you play an instrument or sing, then you will need two things: the files in PDF format and an app to display and organize them.

- Convert your music files to PDF.
- Format for viewing on your iPad.

Converting to PDF

PDF stands for portable document format and is a file format that was created by Adobe when the Internet started to become popular. It is a format that can be read by web browsers and apps. For more information on PDF files consult www.adobe.com/products/acrobat/adobepdf.html.

Some files that you will download and/or purchase may already be in PDF format. If this is the case, you don't need to do anything other than upload them onto your iPad. However, if you want to use other file types, such as word processing files from Microsoft Word, Apple's Pages, or files created on music notation software such as Finale or Sibelius, then you will need to convert these files to PDF before organizing them on your iPad.

Creating PDF Files on Your Computer

You will likely want to convert file formats that are not PDF on your Mac or Windows computer. This is relatively easy to do. Let's look at Mac and Windows options.

Converting to PDF on a Mac Computer

The conversion process for converting any document to PDF is built into the Mac operating system. Follow these steps:

1. Launch the application, and open the file you want to convert.
2. Choose File > Print.
3. Click the PDF button at the bottom of the Mac print window, and choose "Save as PDF."
4. Save the file to a memorable location or folder on your computer's hard drive.

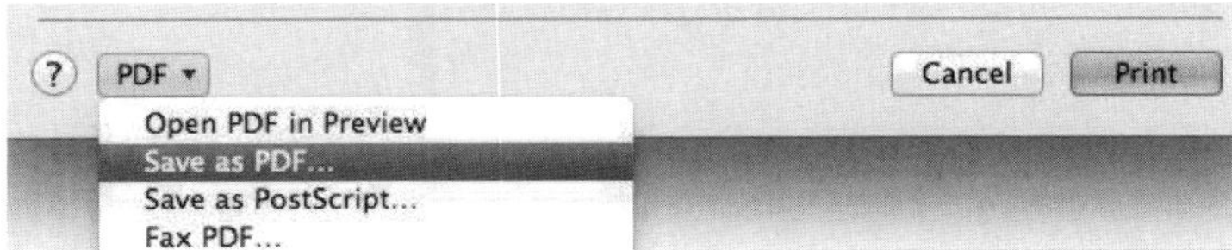

Figure 4.2.

Since you will be moving the files from your computer to your iPad, a process that will be detailed later in this chapter, you should organize them in folders or subfolders in a location you can remember for later access.

Converting to PDF on a Windows Computer

In Windows XP, Windows 7, and Windows 8, you will need to download a PDF creator. There are free options, as well as ones that charge for their software. However, the free options work quite well.

Free Windows PDF Creator Options

Since Windows does not come with a built-in PDF converter, you will need to download free programs such as:

- PDF Creator: http://sourceforge.net/projects/pdfcreator/.
- PrimoPDF: www.primopdf.com/.
- Nitro Reader: www.nitroreader.com/.

After you install the program on your Windows Computer:

1. Launch the application, and open the file you want to convert.
2. Choose File > Print.
3. Choose the PDF writer that you downloaded.
4. Save the file to a memorable location or folder on your computer's hard drive.

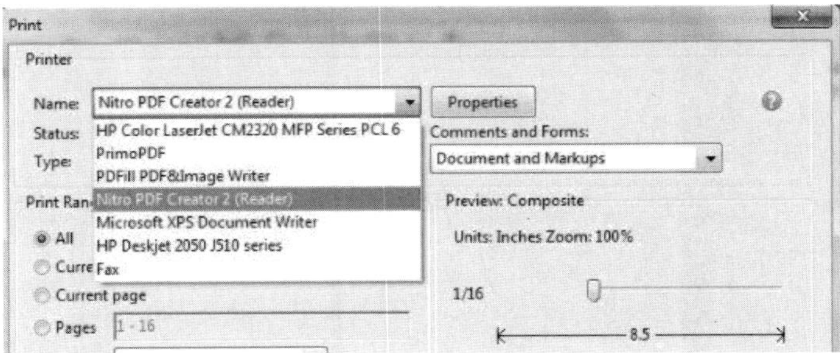

Figure 4.3.

VIDEO 4.1. SAVING IN PDF ON MAC.

Figure 4.4.
http://youtu.be/_akpX2CT-pQ

Windows and Mac PDF Creators for a Fee

The other option is to purchase a PDF writer. With purchased programs, you are able to do more with the files, especially with formatting and manipulating the PDF image. If you have to do a lot of cropping pages, then this is an excellent option. There are many programs from which to choose. The best is Acrobat X Pro. Conveniently, there is a student and teacher edition that lists for $119. The full version lists for $449: www.adobe.com/products/acrobatpro.html.

Scanning

What about the existing printed music that you have in sheet music and books? You can use a scanner to scan the pages and then convert them to PDF using the steps outlined previously in this chapter.

Scanners come in all shapes and sizes and can be purchased for under $100. There are many types of scanners. Since you may be scanning music from a book, a flatbed scanner is the best type to purchase. Canon and HP make affordable, high-quality scanners. All-in-one scanners and printers can be used to scan single pages from books and compilations.

Figure 4.5.

If you are scanning pages from a music book or other source, try to remove the top cover of the scanner if possible. Then, place the book over the scanner and put blank white paper around the exposed edges of the scanner top. For more information on flatbed scanners, go to www.wisegeek.com/what-is-a-flatbed-scanner.htm or http://en.wikipedia.org/wiki/Image_scanner.

You can also use copiers to scan to PDF. Copiers are available in a variety of places. Stores such as Kinkos allow you to scan documents directly to a PDF, which can then be moved to your iPad.

> **Tip:** If you are in a hurry, you could always take a digital photograph of a page of music or lyrics using your digital camera or smartphone and then convert it to a PDF for viewing.

Creating PDF Files Using the iPad

You can create PDF files right from your iPad. This can be done from any program that is used to print, including word processing, music notation (see chapter 6), and other apps. Perhaps you have typed up the lyrics for a song in your word-processing software.

Most programs allow you to save files in PDF format. For example, if you are using the program Pages by Apple to create lyrics, you can save the Pages file in PDF format in five easy steps:

1. With the file open in Pages, click the Tools button on the top right of the iPad.

Figure 4.6.

2. Choose "Share and Print."
3. Select Open in Another App.
4. Select the format: PDF.

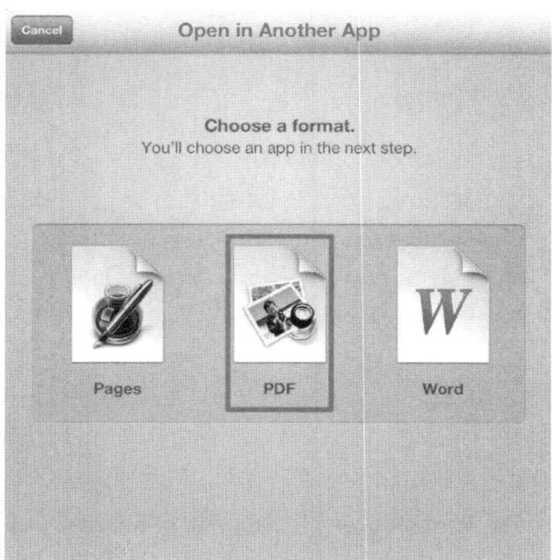

Figure 4.7.

5. Choose the app where you want to associate the saved file.

VIDEO 4.2. SAVING IN PDF ON THE IPAD.

Figure 4.8.
http://youtu.be/4fmdrdR1rdY

PDF Converter Apps

Some apps on the iPad are not as friendly as Pages for saving to PDF. If you find that you need to convert files to PDF format from other applications, then you will need to purchase an app that will make the conversion to PDF.

PDF Converter by Readdle ($6.95)

http://readdle.com/products/pdfconverter/

PDF Converter by Readdle is a well-reviewed app that can save virtually anything on your iPad as a PDF. Viewing music notation on a website and decide you'd like to add it to your song list? Simply use this app to capture the webpage in PDF format.

Save2PDF by EuroSmartz Ltd. ($5.99)

https://itunes.apple.com/us/app/save2pdf/id399758218?mt=8

Save2PDF is another similar app for creating PDF files on your iPad.

Organizing PDF Files

Now that you have your music, lyrics, and other files prepared in PDF format on your computer or iPad, you will want to move them into an app where you can organize your files for viewing, practice, and performance.

iBooks by Apple (Free)

https://itunes.apple.com/us/app/ibooks/id364709193?mt=8

A free option is to move the PDF files into your iPad Library so they will display in the iBooks app that is already loaded on your iPad when you purchase it from Apple. Although iBooks is free and easily accessible, the downside is that it does not have an intuitive way to organize your music. Also, since the app was made for books, it is not the best choice for music. However, if you just want to get started, this is a way to do so, since any PDF file can be added to the app.

Moving the files from your computer to iBooks:

1. Connect your iPad to your computer.
2. Click the Apps tab at the top of the iTunes screen.
3. Under File Sharing in the Apps column, select the app you want to use for organizing and viewing your music files, such as iBooks.
4. Click the Add button to move the files from your computer to your iPad.

VIDEO 4.3. MOVING PDF FILES FROM YOUR COMPUTER TO YOUR IPAD.

Figure 4.9.
http://youtu.be/bbiTRIxfnKM

Organizing Your Music, Lyrics, and Chords

The next step is to select the best music app that will organize and display your music for practice and performance. There are both general apps and ones designed for specific performers.

My Lyric Book by DCTSystems ($1.99)

https://itunes.apple.com/us/app/my-lyric-book/id454781472?mt=8

This app is for vocalists who want to display lyrics that have already been formatted using software or an app exactly as you want them displayed. It supports a wide range of word processing file formats and programs, including Apple Pages, Microsoft Word, and any document in PDF, RTF, or TXT. It is primarily designed for singers, but it also can display music notation in PDF format.

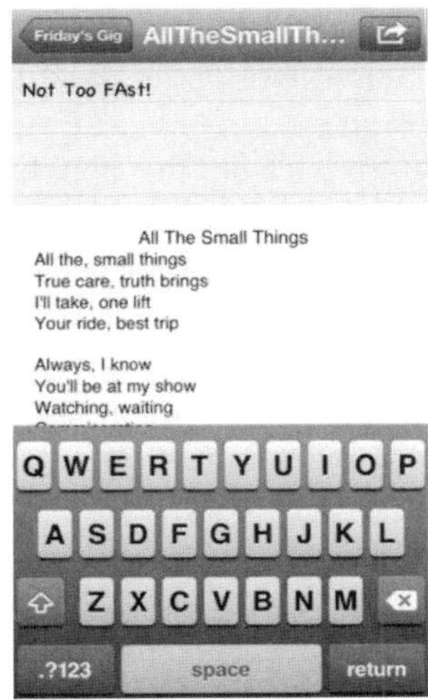

Figure 4.10.

You can also set and save a metronome speed. The metronome has both a sound and a visual prompt, so you can use it as a quick reminder of tempo, even on a noisy stage or in a noisy room.

In addition, you can link lyrics to your iTunes library, so you can refer to a recorded version or play a backing track from within the app through the speakers and headphone on your iPad.

Ultimate Guitar Tabs by Ultimate Guitar ($2.99)

https://itunes.apple.com/us/app/ultimate-guitar-tabs-worlds/id357828853?mt=8

Ultimate Guitar Tabs is an easy and convenient application for viewing guitar tablature, bass tablature, drum tablature, and chords. This app gives you unlimited access to a huge database of tablatures, or tabs, from the Ultimate Guitar website (www.ultimate-guitar.com). You can browse the collection of over 400,000 tabs.

forScore by MGS Development ($4.99)

www.forscoreapp.com

forScore has been around since the inception of the iPad and is one of the most popular apps used by musicians. It is powerful and flexible.

Figure 4.11.

If you are a vocalist or instrumentalist, you definitely want to check out this app. It does it all, from organizing your set lists to linking to an iTunes audio file for playback. This is the program to use for live performance regardless of your instrument.

The list of features is most impressive and includes adding PDF files from other apps on the iPad (including mail attachments), downloading them directly from the web using forScore's browser, and importing and sharing them using your Dropbox account. There is also a built-in storefront so you can search for and purchase free and paid scores that have been optimized for the iPad.

If you have multiple musical roles—perhaps as a performer, educator, and/or church musician—you can use forScore to keep your music organized into neat folders and lists.

With this amazing app, the features go on and on:

- Create a set list for each group to keep your music sorted.
- Need to make a note on a PDF? No problem!
- You can write in rehearsal marks and save them with the document.
- Want to write out some hipper changes for the solo section, or write down a synth-patch number or stage directions? Can do!
- Need to share a score, with your additional notes, and a set list with the rest of your ensemble? Yes, it can do all that too.
- And there's one more thing. You can link any score to an audio file in iTunes (see chapter 1). You can use this to study, practice along, and demo for an ensemble or perform live with prerecorded accompaniment. For more information, check out www.forscoreapp.com/about/.

VIDEO 4.4. VIDEO DEMONSTRATION
BY TRUMPET PLAYER/EDUCATOR ALEX GITTELMAN
USING FORSCORE IN LIVE PERFORMANCE.

Figure 4.12.
http://youtu.be/vN3k6SzzXbY

GigBook by DeepDish ($4.99)

http://deepdishdesigns.com/gigbook.html

This is a robust app and is in competition with forScore. It's worth checking out to see which one you prefer.

Sheet Music Direct for iPad by Hal Leonard Corporation (Free/In-App Purchases Available)

www.halleonard.com

Sheet Music Direct is part storefront, part library, part practice tool, and part performance assistant. You can purchase sheet music in a variety of formats, including piano, piano-vocal, guitar, and choral. Average price for a single title is $3.99. You can view a page of music in preview mode, play an excerpt, and change the key before purchasing. Once purchased, your song is added to your library, which is organized alphabetically by title, artist, or notation (C for choral music, G for guitar music, and so forth), and you can view a listing that displays the first page of the printed score.

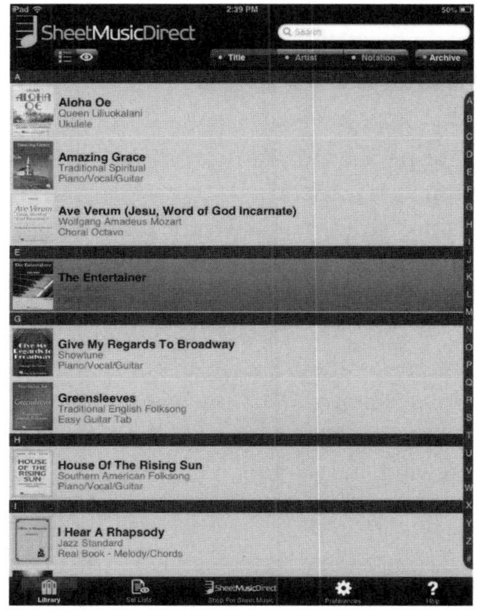

Figure 4.13.

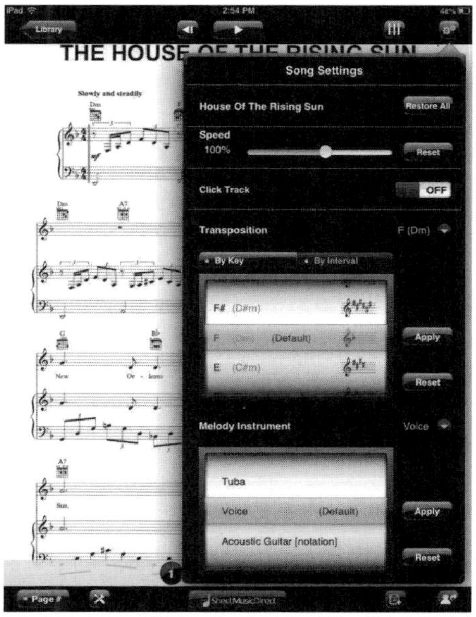

Figure 4.14.

In print view there are several practice tools available to help you learn, including a metronome, a tuner, playback function with mixer, and the ability to change the speed of playback. Other features available on selected pieces include the ability to change key and select a different sound for playback of the melodic line. Page turning via Bluetooth devices is supported; check the app Help file for a list of supported devices.

VIDEO 4.5. SHEET MUSIC DIRECT DEMO.

Figure 4.15.
http://youtu.be/HqXApTBK-dE

Musicnotes Sheet Music Viewer by Musicnotes (Free)

https://itunes.apple.com/us/app/musicnotes-sheet-music-viewer/id369741034?mt=8

This app is designed to work with the www.musicnotes.com website, a digital music download service that offers an incredible number of songs. Some are free, and others can be purchased for a fee in the $4–$5 range, with discounts available when purchasing five or more songs. The company has an immense catalog, with millions of songs from the leading music publishers, including Alfred Music Publishing, Sony/ATV Music Publishing, Disney Music Publishing, BMG, Bourne Music, EMI Music Publishing, Cherry Lane Music Publishing, and many more.

You create an account with Musicnotes on your Mac or Windows computer. Then, when you download music from Musicnotes, your purchases automatically sync with your iPad. The app can be used to organize your songs from this service, including folders and set lists.

Finale and Sibelius Notation Files

Finale (www.finalemusic.com) and Sibelius (www.sibelius.com) are popular computer-based music notation software programs. Computer-based notation software is to music what the word processor is to the written language. Music can be played in via MIDI keyboard or computer keyboard or imported from a MIDI file (see chapter 6). Your file can be anything from a lead sheet to an orchestra score. You can also play back and print scores. Both programs are available for Windows and Macintosh computers.

Sibelius has a variety of computer-based programs available, as does Finale. Finale offers a free computer-based program called Finale Notepad that can affordably and easily be used to create simple scores.

Each company offers an app that allows for viewing and playing files created by the computer-based versions of Finale or Sibelius.

- Finale App: SongBook.
- Sibelius App: Scorch.

SongBook and Scorch Advantages

The main advantage to these apps is that music files can be played back. Unlike PDF files, which can only be viewed, these apps can be used for viewing music and listening to playback with control over the playback tempo. You can also easily add PDF files to these apps.

Also, a composer or arranger with a library of files created in Sibelius or Finale will be able to bring these files to the iPad (notation software users, be patient, we'll get to your app in chapter 6). Unlike with the PDF viewers mentioned earlier in this chapter, documents do not have to be saved in a new format to work with the iPad app.

SongBook and Scorch Disadvantages

You cannot create a new file or edit the notation of files in the current versions of both iPad apps. You also can't generate a PDF file. However, you can create PDF files from the computer-based programs, Finale or Sibelius, and move them to your iPad for viewing.

Both SongBook and Scorch are stand-alone apps. In other words, the files can't be combined with forScore or GigBook unless they are converted to PDF using the computer-based software.

> **Tip:** if you want to use your Finale or Sibelius scores in forScore or GigBook, you can print a PDF version and include the PDF files. However, if you want to play back and manipulate the music, you will need to use the respective notation software app. Keep in mind that these two approaches must be viewed in different apps on your iPad. So if you want to use your iPad primarily in live performance, and playback is not a major issue, then go with the PDF storage format covered earlier in this chapter.

VIDEO 4.6. DEMONSTRATION OF HOW TO CONVERT A COMPUTER SIBELIUS/FINALE FILE INTO PDF FORMAT.

Figure 4.16.
http://youtu.be/dFThWNdGHEc

> **Tip:** If you use the computer-based music notation program Sibelius, you can use the Avid Scorch app to display the files, play back, and change the key on the iPad.

Avid Scorch ($1.99)

https://itunes.apple.com/us/app/avid-scorch/id436394592?mt=8

Avid, the company that produces the notation program Sibelius, has adapted Scorch, their web-viewer technology, to be the engine for their iPad app. This app is ideally suited for viewing and playing back music that was created in Sibelius (www.sibelius.com).

In addition to viewing the music, the file can be played back at any tempo. A metronome click can be turned on or off, making it an ideal practice app. One of the unique features of Scorch is the ability to transpose any song instantly while viewing it on the iPad.

The app is excellent for playing or viewing a specific piece; however, it does not currently support grouping music together in sets, so using it for multiple songs will mean loading each song individually, which is not ideal for live performance.

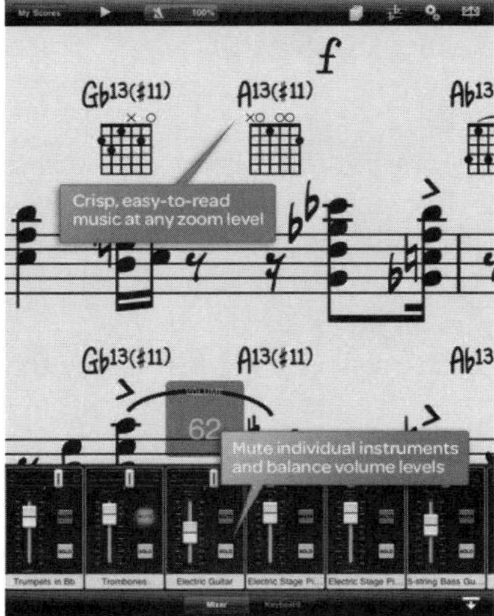

Figure 4.17.

Scorch: Main Screen

The main screen for Scorch looks similar to iBooks, but with a darker wood stain, and the song files are arranged as books with the covers facing out. The app comes with nine sample files, four Sibelius files, and sample pieces from five published folios. There is also one document that functions as the manual. Just as with Sibelius, a tool bar is present with program controls and a Search window.

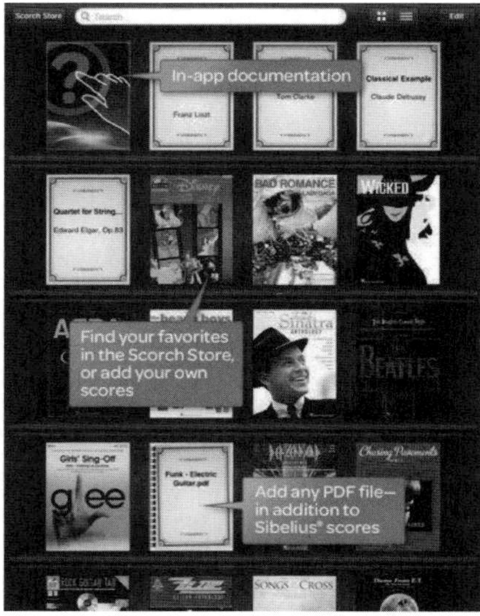

Figure 4.18.

Scorch: Transferring Documents

Documents created and saved by the computer-based version of Sibelius can be transferred to the iPad via iTunes (see chapter 1). iTunes can be used both to load and remove music from the app's library, posting the file in a shared Dropbox folder or attached to an e-mail document.

VIDEO 4.7. VIDEO DEMO OF USING SCORCH ON THE IPAD.

Figure 4.19.
http://youtu.be/IYAHzXCNovA

Tip: If you use the computer-based music notation program Finale, you can use the SongBook app to display and play back your files on the iPad.

SongBook for Finale (Free)

https://itunes.apple.com/us/app/finale-songbook/id529531809?mt=8

MakeMusic, the company that produces Finale, also produces an app called SongBook. So if you are a Finale user, this is a good app to consider.

Launching the app opens the main Library window. Titles are displayed in alphabetical order according to the title of the piece.

A Search box at the top can help locate a file in a long list, and tabs located at the bottom of the window allow you to reorder: by composer, displayed under the title; or by file name, displayed along the right margin. Both options will still be alphabetical. To open a document, tap anywhere in the block that contains the name, composer, and file name.

Set lists can be organized for a variety of applications. So if you have all of your music files in this format and the app, you could use it for live performance as well as for practice.

The tempo can also be manipulated and a metronome sound turned on or off.

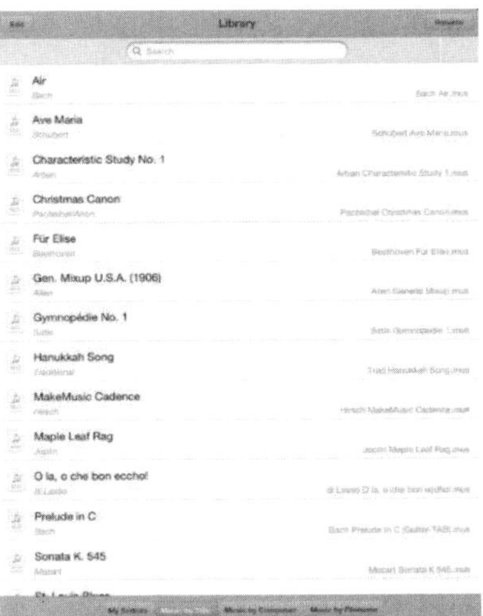

Figure 4.20.

VIDEO 4.8. VIDEO DEMO OF HOW TO USE AND NAVIGATE THE SONGBOOK APP.

Figure 4.21.
http://youtu.be/mrf3cTGqmZ8

Sound Quality

With both the Avid Scorch and Finale SongBook apps, the sound playback is not as high quality as what is available on the computer versions of Finale and Sibelius. However, since the iPad is being used as a portable way to view and listen to files, it fits a specific need.

Getting Files to Your iPad

As with other iPad apps, files can be transferred using iTunes. Other options include attaching the file or files to an e-mail document, or uploading the file to a cloud application such as Dropbox. Be aware that the app determines where it can save files, so each app may not have the same options. iTunes and e-mail are pretty much standard ways to send files to the iPad.

Music Stands

What more could you ask for? How about a place to tee up your iPad so you can actually play your instrument? Now that you are ready to scan all your music and consign those massive fake books to a box in the attic, you'll need something to hold the music at the proper height and angle while you play. There are many stands and cases that can function as stands already available, and new products appear on the market as more uses for the iPad take it into new environments.

The iPad Smart Cover (see chapter 1) is the stand/case combination most will be familiar with, but it favors landscape (sideways) orientation, and most music pages are formatted for portrait (tall) viewing. Most musicians will prefer one of the options designed specifically for musicians.

iKlip Studio ($29.99)

www.ikmultimedia.com/products/iklipstudio/

If your setup, or workspace, has room for a desktop stand, the iKlip from IK Multimedia can hold the iPad in either portrait or landscape orientation. The angle is adjustable, and it folds flat for easy packing and transport. If you use the same manufacturer's iRig, there is the added bonus of a detachable bracket to hold your iRig in place behind the iPad so it doesn't dangle.

Figure 4.22. iKlip Studio.

Desktop stands are also available by other computer accessory makers such as Griffiin, Targus, and Belkin.

Joy Factory Tournez Retractable Clamp Mount ($149.95)

www.thejoyfactory.com/product/aab106

If desk space is at a premium, a clamp mount stand such as the Joy Factory Tournez Retractable Clamp Mount is worth considering, as it can be connected to a table and adjusted for height and visibility.

Figure 4.23.

Stands for Studio and Live Performance

For studio and live performance, there are a number of iPad mounts that clamp onto a mic stand and can position the iPad to be viewed in either portrait or landscape orientation. Prices are in the $40 range for this type of mount. Before purchasing, make sure to check that the bracket supports your iPad model, as there is a subtle difference in thickness between the models currently available.

K&M iPad Stands

company website: http://www.k-m.de/en/

iPad products: http://www.k-m.de/en/search/search/bereich/produkte?q=iPad
K&M offer a line of stands. Be careful when selecting them, as some are specifically designed for specific iPad models. The K&M iPad 2 Mic Stand Holder ($44.99) turns the stand or boom stand into a dedicated iPad music stand.

Figure 4.24.

Standzout Telescoping Floor Stand ($99.95)

www.standzout.com/

Standzout offers a dedicated floor stand if you don't have a mic stand to repurpose, but it is best suited for studio or home use, as it is not easily portable.

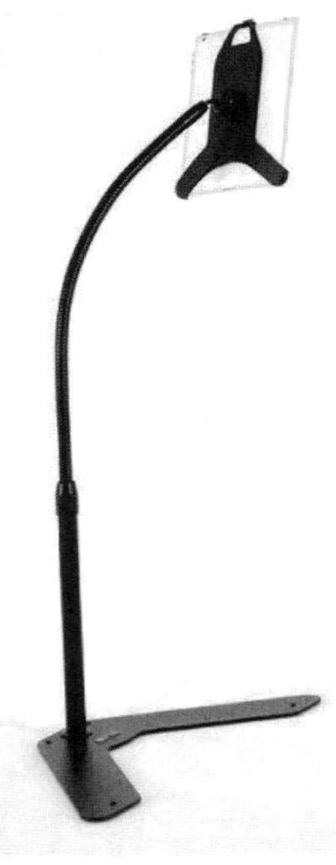

Figure 4.25.

Ultimate Support HyperPad 5 in 1 Stand ($69.99)

www.ultimatesupport.com/product/HYP-100B

If your iPad usage fits all of the above criteria and you need something that can be used in multiple ways, consider Ultimate Support's offering. It provides the hardware for three different mountings, so you'll have everything you need to begin performing.

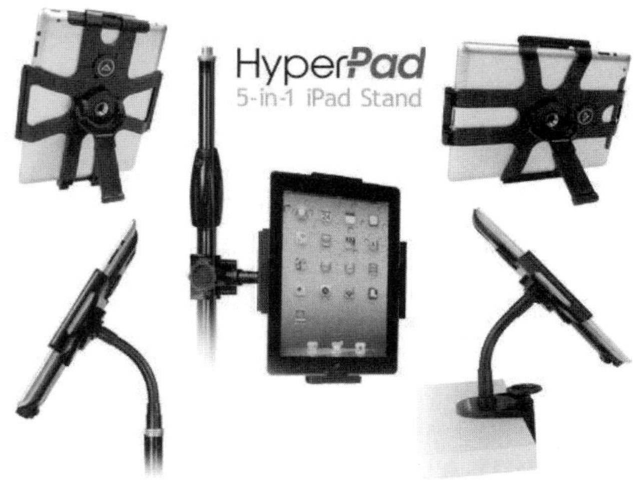

Figure 4.26.

> **Tip:** For using the iPhone on stage or in the studio, Primacoustic offers the Telepad, a mic stand clamp for mounting an iPhone. This allows your phone to be a tuner, lyric prompter, or recording device.

Page Turners

Well, there's just one more thing. In order to turn pages using an iPad, you have two options: use your hand or purchase a foot pedal. For instruments that require both hands, a foot-controlled page turner is recommended.

PageFlip Cicada ($89.99)

www.pageflip.com/pageflip_cicada.html

The PageFlip Cicada is a Bluetooth 3.0 device that can run on batteries or AC power. The unit has two pedals, one for forward turns and one for backward turns. The range for wireless communication is 10 meters, and with Bluetooth pairing it is possible to control multiple units on stage or in the studio with no conflicts. The unit is also compatible with computers, so you can use it with your Bluetooth-enabled desktop or laptop machine.

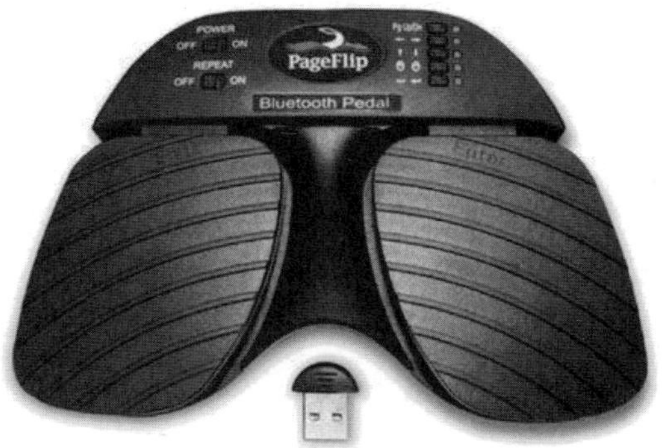

Figure 4.27.

AirTurn BT105 ($119.95) (Includes Two Footswitches)

http://airturn.com/

The AirTurn BT 105 is actually three separate pieces: a Bluetooth transmitter unit that also houses the rechargeable battery, and two footswitches for turning forward and backward. The footswitches are "mechanism free" devices for silent operation in acoustic settings, such as in the studio recording or at live concerts. The battery is capable of 100 hours of operation and is charged via USB. The device can be used with computers as well as the iPad. AirTurn also markets iPad stands and offers packages when both are purchased together.

Figure 4.28.

Before purchasing a foot-controlled page turner, check with to be sure it is compatible with your apps.

VIDEO 4.9. DAVID KIM TALKS ABOUT HIS IPAD AND AIRTURN

Figure 4.29.
http://youtu.be/oD4Gnply4K0

Chapter 4 Activities

1. Open a document in Apple Pages or another word processing program. Save the file in PDF format and associate it with one or more of your iPad apps.
2. Choose one of the apps presented in this chapter for organizing your songs, lyrics, or other PDF files. Use your computer to move files to the app for viewing.
3. Using Songbook for Finale or Scorch for Sibelius, open a file and make changes to the playback of the app: tempo, key, and any other aspects.
4. Using a computer-based program such as Finale, Finale Notepad (free), or Sibelius, create a file and save it to the appropriate iPad app (Scorch or SongBook).
5. There are several ways to transfer documents to your iPad for a specific app:
   a. Use iTunes connected to a computer.
   b. Send an e-mail with an attachment.
   c. Upload the file to a cloud service such as Dropbox.

Summary

This chapter provided an overview of ways you can use your iPad as a music-reading device for practice and performance. Apps that use PDF versions of music were reviewed, including iBooks, forScore, and GigBook. In addition, apps designed to be used with files from computer-based notation programs Finale and Sibelius were described. The hardware needed to make the iPad a viable tool in live performance includes a variety of stands and hands-free page turners. This chapter hopefully will give you the options and procedures necessary for using your iPad to display, play back, and edit music notation files.

Chapter 5
RECORDING

This chapter focuses on recording audio, software instruments, and loops. Software instruments were covered in chapter 3: "Live Performance." There are apps designed to record one specific aspect, such as audio or loops. Other programs can record multiple sources, including audio, software instruments, and loops. Apps range from the most basic free ones to the more expensive and complex ones.

The apps in this chapter do not use or generate music notation. Music notation apps are covered in chapter 6.

SoundCloud

In chapter 1, the concept of cloud storage was introduced. Cloud storage comes in many different forms. One specific cloud option is SoundCloud. Think of SoundCloud (https://soundcloud.com/stream) as part Facebook and part Dropbox. SoundCloud is a social media site, focusing on audio posts that can be finished tracks or works in progress. Other visitors to your SoundCloud page can listen, comment, and if you want, collaborate with you. It can be an excellent place to showcase your work or the work of your students.

You can follow other artists in the same manner as "friending" someone on Facebook and get notifications when they post new material, or just listen to what others are posting. You can search the membership for specific artists or styles of music, and like or post comments on favorite tracks. You can access your account through a web browser or the SoundCloud app. You can also share files posted on SoundCloud, yours or others, through your accounts with Facebook, Twitter, and Tumblr.

SoundCloud (Free)

https://itunes.apple.com/us/app/soundcloud/id336353151?mt=8

Pro and Pro Unlimited service is available for a yearly subscription fee, €29 (€ stands for Euros; there will be a conversion to US dollars when purchased) for Pro, €99 for

Pro Unlimited. With a paid subscription, you can spotlight certain tracks and have them appear at the top of your profile. You'll also have access to data and feedback on your listeners, who they are, and if they are downloading and/or embedding your files. And you can choose to show or hide comments or stats.

> **Tip:** SoundCloud is excellent for posting demos for potential clients to access, freeing you from carrying or mailing physical CDs. You may want to maintain a separate account for this purpose if you also want to post works in progress or work in other genres that doesn't apply to the gig you are trying to land.

VIDEO 5.1. DEMONSTRATION OF SOUNDCLOUD.

Figure 5.1.
http://youtu.be/KddGWc9FNvo

Mono and Stereo Audio Recording

These apps perform the basic task of recording audio. The main focus is recording for the purpose of capturing audio for speech, and they turn your iPad into an audio recorder. You can record a mono signal through the iPad's internal microphone. If you want the greater detail and wider image of a stereo recording, you will need to purchase a stereo microphone that is iOS compatible. Stereo files will take up more space on your device than a mono file at any given resolution.

> **Tip:** *Mono* is a short form of *monaural*. It refers to only one audio channel—as opposed to *stereo*, which means two (usually a left and a right), and *quad*, which means four.

WavePad HD by NCH Software (Free)

www.nch.com.au/wavepad/index.html.

WavePad is a basic mono recorder with some effects and editing capability. Editing is excellent for trimming excess space before and after a recording or to cut and paste sections of a recording. WavePad has settings for a fixed record time, helpful if you need to place the iPad at a distance from the ensemble you are recording. It also has settings for the file type and resolution, and it calculates the amount of time you can record based on available storage in your iPad. WavePad is also available for the iPhone and Mac and PC computers. One of the limits of the current version is that the only way to share files is to e-mail them or use a somewhat cumbersome FTP (file transfer protocol) website. However, the price is right: free.

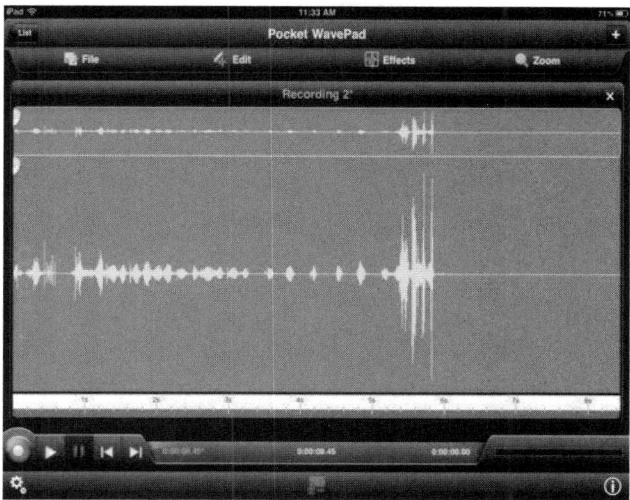

Figure 5.2. WavePad.

Tip: Remember to check the meters before recording. If you are performing something, test the loudest passage to make sure the level is not so loud it distorts.

VIDEO 5.2. WAVEPAD.

Figure 5.3.
http://youtu.be/t_vpcJZ-8EI

Røde Rec by Røde Microphones ($5.99/LE Version: Free)

http://www.rodemic.com/software

Anyone familiar with the FiRe app from Audiofile Engineering will recognize this app. It has been purchased by the Røde Microphones and renamed Røde Rec. The LE version is free and offers broadcast-quality recording functions, as well as the ability to use iTunes file sharing or direct publish to SoundCloud. The paid version adds processing and editing tools, exporting in more audio file formats, and publishing to Dropbox.

The ability to change the recording resolution gives you the option of saving space on your iPad by using a lower sample rate for recording lectures or notes for dictation, and a higher sample rate for music and media work. (See the tip, below.) This app was designed originally for the iPhone but runs on the iPad as well.

Figure 5.4. Røde Rec.

Tip: If you are new to digital audio and some of the terms used in this chapter are not familiar to you, there is an excellent glossary hosted by the Sweetwater company: www.sweetwater.com/insync/category/glossary/. For example, the definition of *sample rate* is in the glossary: http://www.sweetwater.com/insync/sample-rate/.

Stereo Microphones

To use your iPad as a stereo recorder, you will need to purchase a stereo microphone. These microphones plug directly in to the 30-pin port on the iPad.

Mikey Digital by Blue Microphones ($99.99)

http://bluemic.com/mikey_digital/

Mikey Digital is the current version of the original iOS external microphone. Mikey can be used with GarageBand, Multitrack DAW, Jammit (covered in chapter 9), and other recording apps. Mikey also has a 1/8-inch line-in jack allowing you to connect a line source to your iPad. So you could connect any device with a line-out signal, such as a CD player or other audio device. You cannot use the mic and line-in inputs simultaneously. Mikey Digital supports the Apple Lightening Adapter for connecting to iOS devices with Lightening ports.

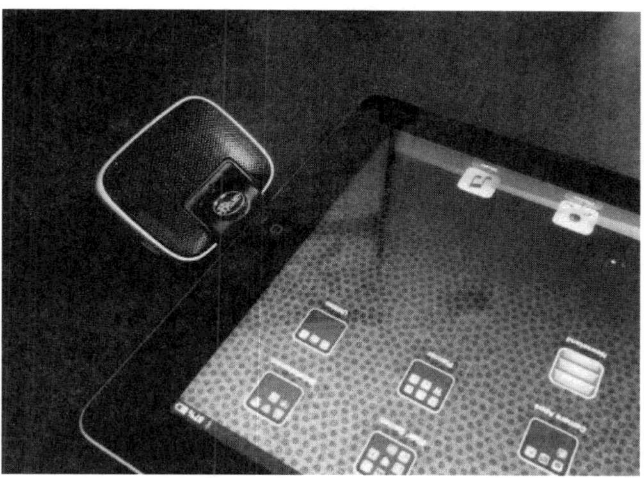

Figure 5.5. Mikey Digital Stereo Microphone.

Røde iXY by Røde ($199)

www.ixymic.com/

The microphone capsules on this unit are set in an X/Y stereo pattern (angled 90% from each other) to provide a stereo image. It can record in resolutions up to 96 kHz/24-bit for maximum fidelity when used with the Røde app. The mic has a built-in high-pass filter to minimize handling noise. For table placement, the iPad, or iPhone, will have an upward tilt due to the width of the microphone's base. If you are shooting video with a DSLR camera, the iPhone with the iXY mic can be mounted on the camera's flash mount, using a third-party mount, to capture quality audio that can be synched to the video in the computer. The iXY microphone is not compatible with Lightening port iOS devices or the Apple Lightning Adapter.

Figure 5.6. Røde iXY stereo mic.

VIDEO 5.3. RODE IXY MICROPHONE DEMO

Figure 5.7.
http://www.viddler.com/v/2f33cfd8

Tip: If you own an iPhone, the Voice Memos app can be used for capturing anything you can sing, hum, or vocalize.

Multitrack Audio Recording

While many of the apps mentioned thus far in this chapter are excellent music creation environments, there comes a time when you may just need an app that's more focused on the process of multitrack recording, which is, literally, the ability to record more than one track. With this software, you can record one item—for example, the vocals—and then go back and add the drums, then the keyboards, and so forth.

The Beatles, and producer George Martin, brought multitrack recording into prominence with the album *Sargent Pepper's Lonely Hearts Club Band* in 1964. That album was recorded on 4 tracks. Since then the race to larger track counts grew to 24 in the analog world and 32 with digital tape. With multitrack DAW (digital audio workstation) software being the norm in music production, working in a multitrack environment from the beginning of the music creation process is the norm. Multitrack software provides the ability to record, edit, and work through to the final mix in the same document of the same program.

MultiTrackDAW by Harmonicdog (\$9.99/In-App Purchases Available)

www.harmonicdog.com

The name says it all. It is a multitrack digital audio workstation. Digital audio workstations are referred to as DAWs, having some ability to record, manipulate, and play back audio recordings and record in multiple tracks. The only option in this app is to record audio. The current version does not support recording software instruments or loops. There are effects available for processing it. It comes with 8-track capacity, which can be upgraded to 24 with an in-app purchase.

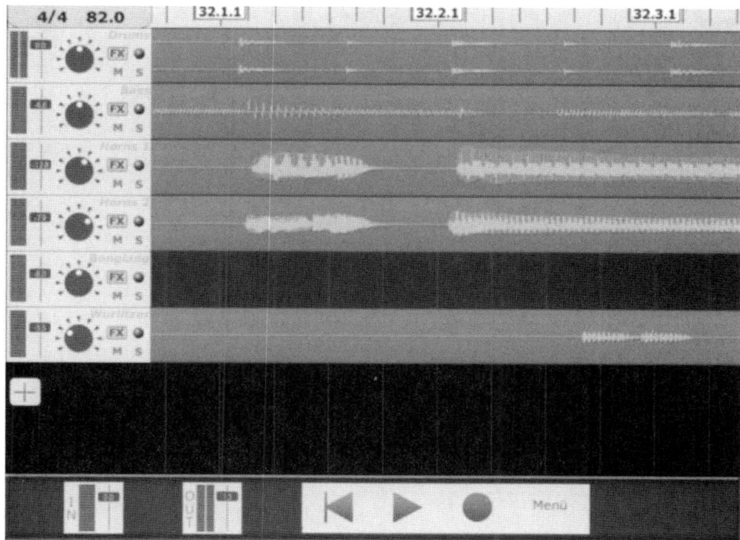

Figure 5.8. MultiTrackDAW.

Figure 5.9.

Auria by WaveMachine Labs Inc. ($24.99 and $49.99 Versions)

http://auriaapp.com/

Auria has made a big splash as the "Pro Tools" of the iPad." If you are unfamiliar with the term *Pro Tools*, check out http://en.wikipedia.org/wiki/Pro_Tools.

At $49.99 it is an expensive app. That's not to say it isn't a good deal for what it can do, but if you don't need its power, Auria LE at $24.99 might be better suited for demo recording, rehearsal recording, or live-event recording. The LE version has 8 tracks of simultaneous recording instead of 24, and 24 tracks of playback instead of 48. Some effects plug-ins are included and others available as in-app purchases. Should you decide you need all the power of the full version, you can upgrade at any time as an in-app purchase.

Figure 5.10. Auria Mixer.

Figure 5.11.

Figure 5.12.

VIDEO 5.4 AURIA MULTITRACK.

Figure 5.13.
http://www.youtube.com/watch?v=vnkFDM65jjw&feature=share&list=PL5C9EF8A1E64F939C

Loop Recording

A *loop* is a sound that continually repeats itself over and over again. In the 1980s and '90s, looping became an art form, and quite often loops would make or break sounds used in digital instruments. In recent years, audio loops of entire musical passages have become very popular. A looped rhythm section, for example, can be an excellent foundation for another tune or arrangement.

Loops can be created in apps that are dedicated to this technique, or they can be combined in DAW programs so that you can record audio and loops in the same program. Both of these methods will be reviewed in this chapter.

Loop Apps

Everyday Looper by Mancing Dolecules ($5.99)

www.mancingdolecules.com/

Everyday Looper provides up to six tracks of loop recording for sampling instruments, vocal beatbox tracks, or anything else you can record.

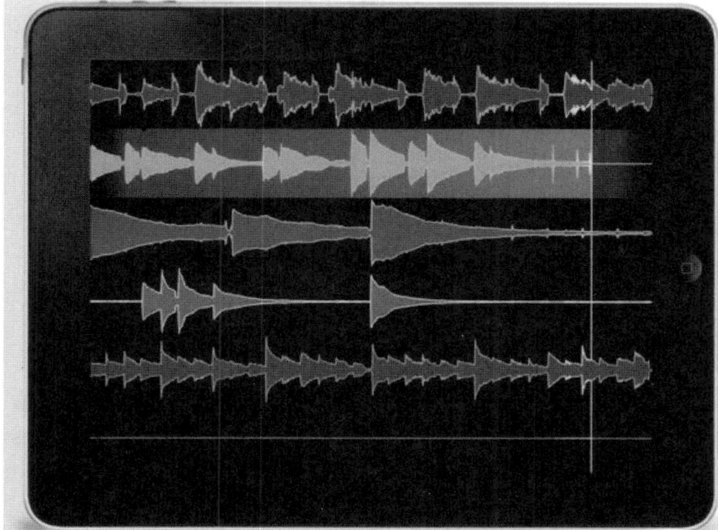

Figure 5.14. Everyday Looper.

Loopy HD by A Tasty Pixel ($7.99)

http://loopyapp.com/

Loopy HD has the most unique interface, looking like a grid of Lifesaver candies. Is it any wonder the app is made by a company called A Tasty Pixel? It provides up to 12 tracks of loops, which you can use to create more complex textures. Loopy can also import loops in a number of different audio formats, including the popular AIFF, WAV, MP3, M4A, and others.

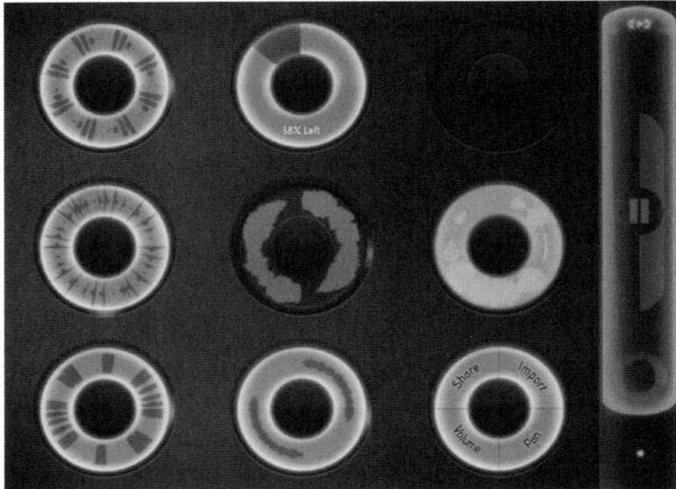

Figure 5.15. Loopy HD.

VIDEO 5.5. LOOPY HD.

Figure 5.16.
http://youtu.be/BtZcYBgRVEs

Digital Audio Workstation Apps

The next and most powerful app category can record audio, loops, and software instruments. You can record in multiple tracks and include one or all of the elements: audio, software instruments, and/or loops. The software also assists with the mixdown of the tracks into one audio file that you can share with others.

GarageBand by Apple Inc. ($4.99)

www.apple.com/apps/garageband/

GarageBand on the iPad is the Swiss army knife of music production (DAW). In addition to handling MIDI data and prerecorded loops, it can record audio from external sources, such as vocals and guitars, and audio from internal sources, such as software synths.

The many software instruments available in GarageBand were reviewed in chapter 3: "Live Performance." What was not discussed in chapter 3 was that each of these instruments can be recorded onto one or more tracks. And you can also record live audio and manipulate loops. If you want to get an idea down without technology getting in the way, it's hard to top GarageBand on the iPad.

> **Tip:** Be aware that on a scale of 1 to 10, GarageBand on the iPad is around a 2 or 3. On a Mac, it is approximately a 4 or 5. There are other more powerful DAW programs for Mac and Windows such as Logic, Pro Tools, and Cubase, which take you to a 10. Being aware of the capabilities and limitations of these apps is important.

Recording GarageBand Software Instruments

In chapter 3, you looked at the instruments available in GarageBand that can be used for live performance. All of these instruments can be recorded onto a track and edited. You can record a performance and then correct notes or adjust the notes and rhythms you recorded. The current version of GarageBand allows you to record up to eight discrete tracks. And GarageBand will help aid your performance by automatically adjusting the timing or quantizing as you record.

VIDEO 5.6. RECORDING GARAGEBAND SOFTWARE INSTRUMENTS AND QUANTIZING.

Figure 5.17.
http://youtu.be/wrCnHtYb6Fo

Expanding with a MIDI Keyboard

As was mentioned in chapter 3, a MIDI keyboard can be connected to the iPad and used to input software instruments into a GarageBand track. Plug the USB cable from the keyboard into the iPad Camera Connector (sold separately).

VIDEO 5.7. RECORDING GARAGEBAND WITH AN EXTERNAL MIDI KEYBOARD.

Figure 5.18.
http://youtu.be/grfZjxlJaZ4

Expanding GarageBand Instruments

Chapter 3 also featured a lot of non–GarageBand instruments and synthesizers that can now be used with GarageBand, thanks to Audiobus, the app that can connect the output of those instruments with GarageBand's inputs. This greatly expands your available sound pallet and will help your music move beyond the sound of GarageBand's internal instruments. See chapter 3 for the specifics on using Audiobus.

Recording Audio in GarageBand

GarageBand can be used to record mono and stereo audio. It can be used as your audio recording source. You don't have to include software instruments if you don't want to. GarageBand, like the other multitrack audio apps reviewed earlier in this chapter, can record audio. You can record one mono or stereo track or multiple tracks of audio.

VIDEO 5.8. RECORDING AUDIO IN GARAGEBAND.

Figure 5.19.
http://youtu.be/AOgZ6zvavws

Recording Loops in GarageBand

GarageBand makes it very easy to work with loops. Loops are automatically matched to the key and tempo of your project. You can audition loops and then drag them into the GarageBand project window. GarageBand will create a track for the loop if one does not exist. Loops can be a great way to get an instant drum groove entered or add other parts of the song such as bass, guitar, sound effects, and more.

VIDEO 5.9. CREATING LOOP TRACKS IN GARAGEBAND.

Figure 5.20.
http://youtu.be/6AIFs_oAE3o

Tip: Mac Users: If you own a Mac desktop or laptop machine and want to expand your collection of Apple loops beyond the collection included with GarageBand, check MainStage in the computer's App Store. MainStage is the software-synth side of Logic, minus the sequencer and recording capability. It comes with access to 19 GB of loops and samples that can be downloaded from inside the app and is included in the $29.99 purchase price. These loops can be transferred to the iOS versions of GarageBand using iTunes.

VIDEO 5.10. GARAGEBAND WITH AUDIOBUS SETUP.

Figure 5.21.
http://youtu.be/1aa2yqk5Lw0

Tip: While you can begin a song on GarageBand for iPad and transfer it to GarageBand on the Mac, you cannot transfer a song from GarageBand on the Mac to your iPad.

It's possible to link up to three iOS devices running GarageBand together over Wi-Fi or Bluetooth for Jam Sessions. One device must be designated as the band leader, which will also be the recording device. You can use any of GarageBand's instruments, live instruments, or vocals.

VIDEO 5.11. JAM SESSION SETUP.

Figure 5.22.
http://youtu.be/TseMYXU47Ww

Song files can be transferred off the iPad through iTunes file transfer and e-mail. You can export audio files to Facebook, YouTube, SoundCloud, and iMove. It is also possible to create and save ringtones on the iPad in GarageBand. There is also the option to export a song file in GarageBand format that can be opened on another iOS device with GarageBand.

VIDEO 5.12. EXPORTING FILES.

Figure 5.23.
http://youtu.be/SM6C1RX0Jgo

Cubasis by Steinberg Media Technologies GmbH ($49.99)

www.steinberg.net/en/products/ios_apps/cubasis.html

Cubase is the first of the major DAW desktop apps to have an iOS version available. Though limited to CD-quality resolution, it can handle audio, with editing and effects, plus MIDI that can drive any MIDI device. Connecting MIDI devices is covered at the end of this chapter.

If you use Cubase on a desktop machine, the look and feel will be familiar. Audio track count will depend on your model of iPad. Sixty-four tracks are possible with the fourth-generation iPad and iPad Mini.

VIDEO 5.13. CUBASIS.

Figure 5.24.
http://youtu.be/kc4mXBevOE8

FL Studio Mobile HD by Image Line Software ($19.99/In-App Purchases Available)

www.image-line.com/documents/flstudiomobile.html

FL Studio Mobile HD also traces its roots back to the desktop computing environment. If you already own the desktop version, the similarity will make using this app a snap. In-app purchases are available to add additional instruments and drum kits. You can create your own custom drum kits. Audio files can be cut, trimmed, normalized, reversed, and faded in or out with your choice of three different curves.

Figure 5.25.

Figure 5.26.

VIDEO 5.14. FL STUDIO OVERVIEW.

Figure 5.27.
http://youtu.be/0Q-AoN2q9qE

NanoStudio by Blip Interactive Ltd. ($13.99/In-App Purchases Available)

www.blipinteractive.co.uk/

NanoStudio combines a synth, drum pads, a mixer, effects and a sampler and sample editor, which gives it a unique edge. Expanding the number of available tracks from 6 to 16 is a $4.99 in-app purchase. If you like to work with samples, this app may be a tool worth exploring.

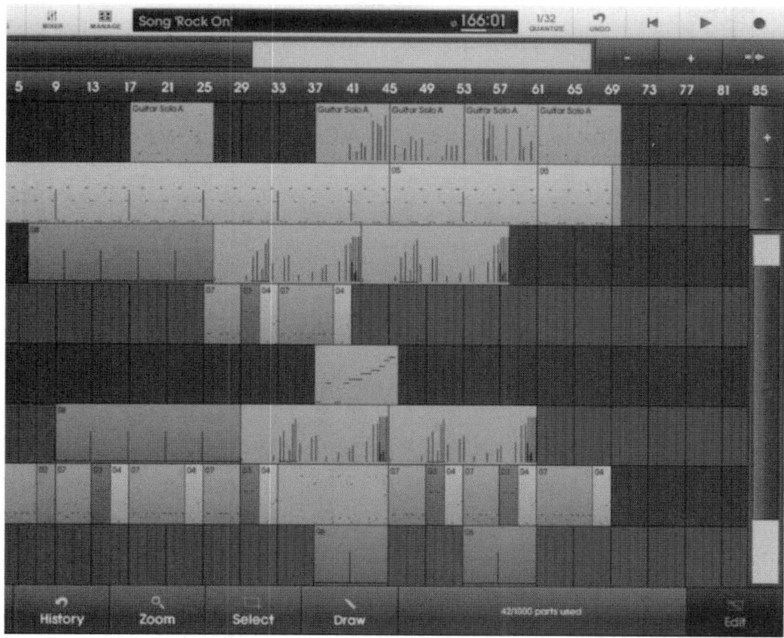

Figure 5.28.

Figure 5.29.

Special-Purpose Apps

These apps were created for specific instruments or the voice. They have multitrack recording capability but are more suited for recording multiple tracks of the instrument for which each is designed.

AmpliTube for iPad by IK Multimedia (Free/$11.99)

www.ikmultimedia.com/products/amplitubeipad/

Though AmpliTube is first and foremost a guitar amp and effects pedal emulator, it has the ability to record its output internally. With an in-app purchase, single-track capability can be expanded to eight tracks. It has a drum loop module to keep time as you build bass and guitar parts on top to create your track. Add vocals, and use the Master FX to create a complete track. There are a few variations on this title available in the App Store, one that reproduces the Fender amp tone and two that replicate the sound of Slash and Jimi Hendrix.

Figure 5.30.

Figure 5.31.

VIDEO 5.15. AMPLITUBE.

Figure 5.32.
http://youtu.be/bjtSnG22Qp8

VocaLive by IK Multimedia (Free/$19.95)

www.ikmultimedia.com/products/vocaliveipad/

Vocalists can use the in-app purchase in VocaLive to add eight-channel recording capability to the suite of popular vocal effects in the app and create complex vocal arrangements or simply alternate versions of a basic vocal.

Figure 5.33.

Figure 5.34.

VIDEO 5.16. VOCALIVE.

Figure 5.35.
http://youtu.be/kZm--fhaxCo

Electronic Music Apps

Figure and iKaossilator are two apps designed for dance and electronica styles of music, and to be used on mobile devices. Each design represents a unique approach to controlling sound.

Figure by Propellerhead Software ($0.99)

http://www.propellerheads.se/products/figure/

Figure is produced by Propellerhead Software AB, also the company that makes the Mac and PC software Reason. The app is designed for creating music in the mobile environment. Using a nonconventional interface, controls are designed for fingers or thumbs on the screen, and they do not attempt to replicate the look of a hardware device. It is best suited for electronica and dance styles, so it's not for everyone, but it offers a unique approach to music creation.

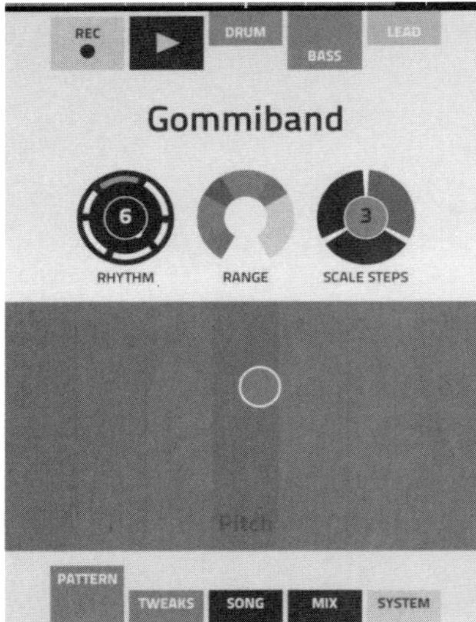

Figure 5.36.

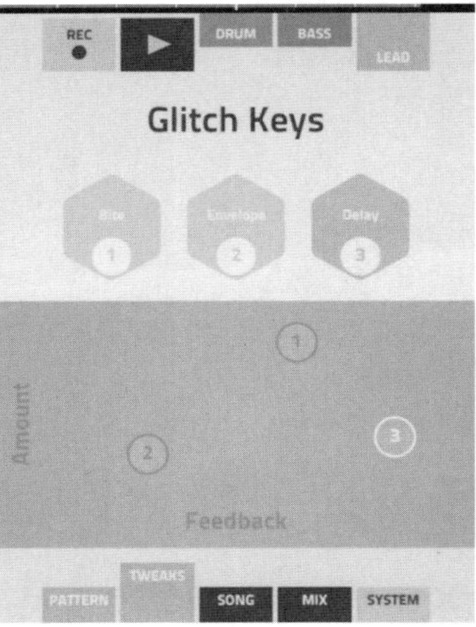

Figure 5.37.

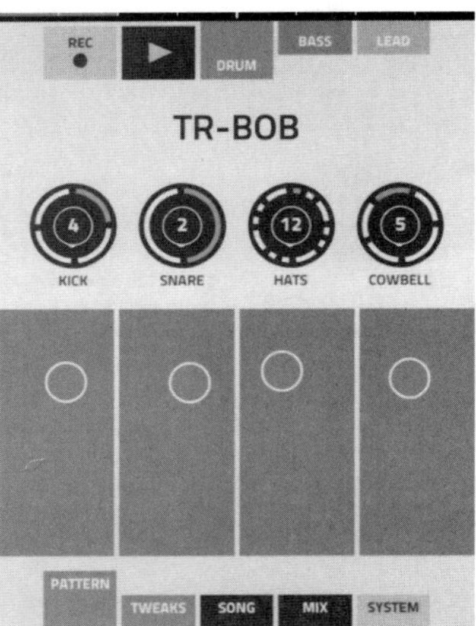

Figure 5.38.

VIDEO 5.17. FIGURE FOR IPHONE.

Figure 5.39.
http://youtu.be/gLLjRH6GJec

iKaossilator by Korg ($19.99)
www.korg.com/ikaossilator

The Kaossilator is an X–Y pad instrument that lets you control up to five musical parts on a single pad. This is also a dance or electronica instrument with sounds suited to hip-hop, house, techno, dubstep, nu-disco, and electro styles. All it takes is one finger, and you are off and running.

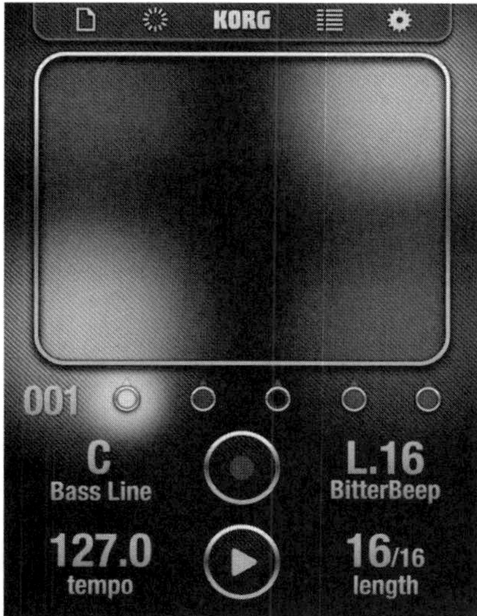

Figure 5.40.

Figure 5.41.

> **Tip:** The website www.iosmusician.com maintains a list of apps for the iOS platform. A valuable tool in itself, but don't miss the sidebar on the right side of the page. They track apps that are on sale, have been reduced in price, or have limited-time promotional pricing.

File Management

All of the apps mentioned in this chapter offer the same file management options discussed in chapter 1: synching with iTunes to transfer song files to your computer or upload to Dropbox or SoundCloud. These methods take time and some form of connection, either to a computer or Wi-Fi, so take advantage of breaks, meals, sleep, or any other downtime you have. Even with the most robust iPad (currently 128 GB), you will fill it up sooner or later.

If you record with a number of different apps, you will have files for the same project in several places on your iPad. Since you can't access the files directly in the iOS interface, the only way to access them is through the app that created the file. In the desktop computing world, files are visible and easily managed in the Mac and Windows OS. Enter an app called AudioShare.

AudioShare by Kymatica (Jonatan Liljedahl) ($3.99)

https://itunes.apple.com/us/app/audioshare-audio-document/id543859300?mt=8

This app allows you to organize, edit, import, and export any audio and MIDI files on your iPad. Organization involves creating folders and renaming and transferring files between apps or to your computer or cloud storage. It also can record sound from an external source. Export options are to iTunes, either by e-mail or by uploading to Dropbox and downloading the file on a desktop or laptop computer.

VIDEO 5.18. FILE MANAGEMENT.

Figure 5.42.
http://youtu.be/2-Qii6ZMgsE

Importing and Exporting Data

There are many options for exporting and importing data from the iPad, which include the following.

- Dropbox (and Other Similar Services, Such as Google Drive and Skydrive): Wireless transfer to cloud storage that works both as a backup and to share with collaborators and bandmates. Requires an Internet connection, preferably Wi-Fi, so you don't chew up cellular-data allowances.
- E-Mail Transfer: Wireless transfer of data. Be aware of file-size limits that may be imposed by your Internet service provider. If you are transferring large files, this may not be an option. E-mail is an excellent choice for personal backups or transferring files to a desktop app for further work.
- iTunes Sync: Backs up directly to and from your computer with a wired connection. Works best for personal backups, or transferring files to or from a desktop app for further work.
- SoundCloud: A way to post audio files for sharing with anyone and everyone.

Tip: Back up your iPad frequently, especially before beginning a recording session. If you've been downloading a lot of apps and loading up on media content such as movies, you may be risking a memory crisis once you start recording. If this happens, delete any video files you may have in iTunes, as they take up the most space. Audio files in iTunes can also be deleted. If you still need space, you can delete nonessential apps and reload them later. iTunes tracks which media and apps you've purchased or downloaded, so you can easily redownload any media files from iCloud, and any apps from the App app after your recording session is finished.

Activities

1. Record mono audio using one of the apps in this chapter. After you record it:
   a. Trim the silences from the beginning and ends.
   b. Normalize it.
   c. Export it via e-mail or another option.
2. Open an MP3 file of a recording into a recording app. Trim and edit the file.
3. Create a rhythm section groove using just loops.
4. Using one of the DAW apps such as GarageBand, create a project that includes software instruments, audio, and loops.
5. Using a practice app such as iReal b (chapter 7), export a MIDI file and import it into GarageBand or a similar app.

Summary

This chapter covered the various ways to record sound with the iPad, including mono and stereo audio, multitrack, loops, and DAW (digital audio workstation) software. Storing audio using SoundCloud was addressed. Special-purpose apps designed for recording the voice or specific instruments were included, as well as apps geared toward electronic-music recording and production.

Chapter 6
Composing and Songwriting with Notation

Chapter 4 dealt with displaying music notation for reading and performance. Chapter 5 took you through the apps for composing with sound using loops and audio. In this chapter, we will review the options for composing music with notation on the iPad.

Notation Software Overview

Aura Lee

Figure 6.1. Music notation sample.

There are two main categories of composition with the iPad: composing with sound and composing with notation. In this chapter, the focus is on music notation. So the person composing has to have a background in music notation, since that is the medium used for note entry and display.

Finale and Sibelius

The two major players in the computer-based music notation world are Finale (www.finalemusic.com) and Sibelius (www.sibelius.com). Both of these companies have iPad apps available for playing and displaying their files that were reviewed in chapter 4. However, neither company currently offers an iPad app for creating music notation.

So if you want to create notation on your iPad, and you are a Finale or Sibelius user, you will need to use an app by another company and transfer the files to and from the iPad.

File Formats

When exchanging files with different apps, it is important to be aware of the various file types, as some are and some are not compatible with each other. In lesson 1, the native app was discussed. All apps typically create a native app file format that is only able to be read by that specific app.

If you want to exchange files with different music notation apps, you will need to use a file format that is common to both apps.

MIDI Files or Standard MIDI Files

Most music apps reviewed in chapter 5 and in this chapter can save in MIDI file format. MIDI files (also called Standard MIDI Files) transmit performance information such as pitches, rhythms, time signatures, and the like. Text elements such as chord symbols, lyrics, and page-layout formats are not captured in MIDI files.

MIDI files can be very useful when you want to share music files between apps, as was mentioned in chapter 5. Most notation software apps also can import and export MIDI files. This capability is an important feature to consider.

MusicXML

A more sophisticated way to share music notation files is via MusicXML (XML stands for Extensible Markup Language and is used for a wide variety of software applications). MusicXML translates music notation into a language that can be exported and imported between apps. With MusicXML, in addition to the notation, the text elements, page layout, and other elements are also maintained. The translation is not 100% perfect, but often files will translate with 95% or greater accuracy.

If you want to maximize the use of an iPad music notation app, look for apps with the capability of importing and exporting files in both MIDI and MusicXML formats. This will allow you to create a file in one app and then import it into others for further editing.

Tip: For more information on MIDI files check out http://www.midi.org/aboutmidi/. For MusicXML, go to www.musicxml.com/.

Notation App Roundup

Let's begin by reviewing some of the available notation apps. As in other chapters in this book, this list is not exhaustive, but it represents some of the more popular music notation apps available.

Scorio Music Notator by Fun Communications GmbH ($3.99)

https://itunes.apple.com/us/app/scorio-music-notator/id417227998?mt=8

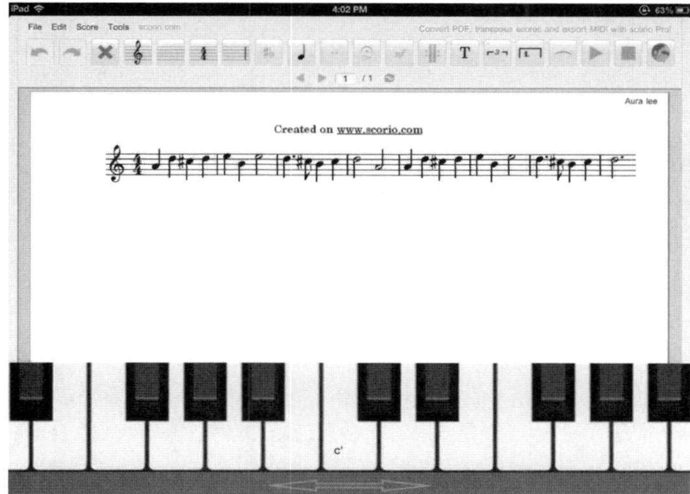

Figure 6.2. Scorio Notation app on the iPad.

Scorio is designed to be used on the iPad to create, modify, and print scores. The added bonus is that you can go to the Scoria website and continue to edit your projects using their web-based editor. You can then save your projects to the Scorio website and work on your projects on your Mac or PC computer by going to the scoria website: www.scorio.com. From there, you can export files in MIDI and MusicXML format. On the website, you can save in MIDI and MusicXML format, but not on the iPad. There are paid subscriptions that add functionality to these apps. Review the options at www.scorio.com/web/scorio/products.

Since the editing options in the app and on the website are somewhat limited, this app is best for basic note entry and not those who work with full scores and arrangements.

VIDEO 6.1. SCORIO APP.

Figure 6.3.
http://youtu.be/6hUcgPRaq2U

iWriteMusic for iPad by iWriteMusicProject ($5.99)

https://itunes.apple.com/us/app/iwritemusic-for-ipad/id466261478?mt=8

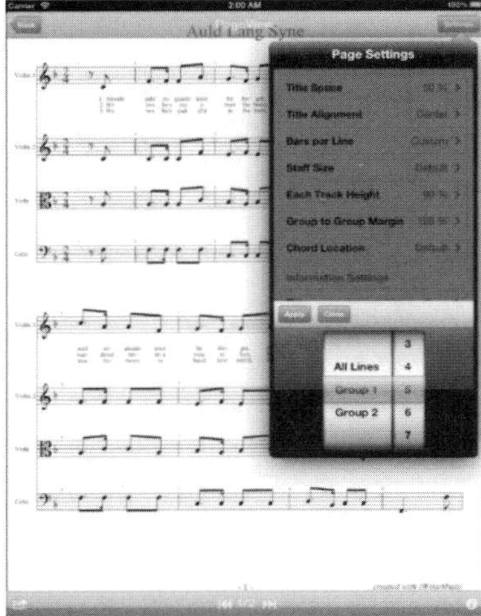

Figure 6.4. iWriteMusic for iPad.

If you are looking for an easy-to-use app for basic music notation creation or for use with students, then consider iWriteMusic. The cost of the app is $5.99, and it can create and print out lead sheets and basic scores. It can share files in MIDI format. Currently MusicXML import/export is not available.

VIDEO 6.2. VIDEO DEMONSTRATION OF IWRITEMUSIC.

Figure 6.5. iWriteMusic for iPad.
www.youtube.com/watch?feature=player_embedded&v=ysj5W4ozpnY#!

Guitar Pro by Arobas Music ($7.99)

https://itunes.apple.com/us/app/guitar-pro/id400666114?mt=8

Guitar Pro is available for iPad, and there are versions for Mac and PC computers. The advantage to using this app is it supports guitar tab (tablature) as well as standard music notation.

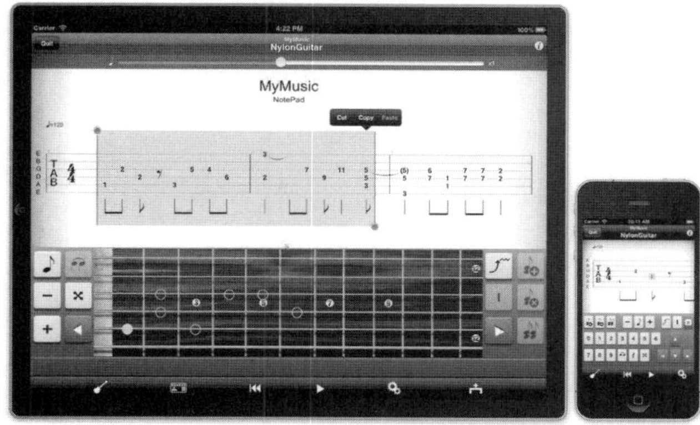

Figure 6.6. Guitar Pro for iPad and iPhone.

VIDEO 6.3. DEMO OF GUITAR PRO.

Figure 6.7. Guitar Pro.
http://youtu.be/uy32sj2KOgs

High-End Notation Apps

There are two apps that I would place in the high end of music notation creation on the iPad. These are:

Symphonix Evolution by Vinclaro ($12.99)

https://itunes.apple.com/us/app/symphonix-evolution/id414192515?mt=8

Notion by NotionMusic ($14.99)

https://itunes.apple.com/us/app/notion/id475820434?mt=8

Both of these apps are pretty robust, as they can create scores in a variety of formats. Of the two, I like Notion best, as it can do all of the basic notation needs, as well as import and export files in a variety of formats, including MIDI and MusicXML.

Figure 6.8. Notion for iPad.

> **Tip:** Another high-end notation option on the iPad is Noteflight (www.noteflight.com). It is not an app, but it works within the Safari web browser.

VIDEO 6.4. NOTION TUTORIALS.

Figure 6.9.
www.notionmusic.com/support/tutorials.html

Notion: Computer and iPad Versions

Notion makes a Mac and a PC version of their software, as well as an iPad app. So if you are interested in working in Notion on both the iPad and your computer, you will have to purchase the computer version and the iPad app: www.notionmusic.com.

> **Tip:** If you are a Sibelius or Finale user on your computer, then you can use the Notion iPad version by exchanging files via MusicXML.

Notion Playback

Notion gives you the ability to compose, edit, and play back scores using real audio samples performed by the London Symphony Orchestra, recorded at Abbey Road Studios in London.

The app comes with some basic sounds built in. You can purchase additional sounds if you want via an in-app purchase.

Figure 6.10. Notion in-app purchase of sounds.

Notion Projects

After installing Notion for iPad, you can create a new score, download scores from the Internet, and import either MIDI or MusicXML scores. You can also use iTunes to transfer files from your computer to the Notion app. The file formats supported include NOTION, which are proprietary files created by Notion Software; MIDI; MusicXML; and GuitarPro 3–5.

Storing and Sharing your Scores

After creating a Notion score, you have a variety of options for sharing and export. You can save the file to the iPad, e-mail it to yourself or someone else, or export the file in MusicXML so you can import it into another program such as Finale or Sibelius. Exporting as MIDI allows you to open it in other music software, and a PDF can be printed out. Dropbox is an option for saving and sharing files using cloud computing.

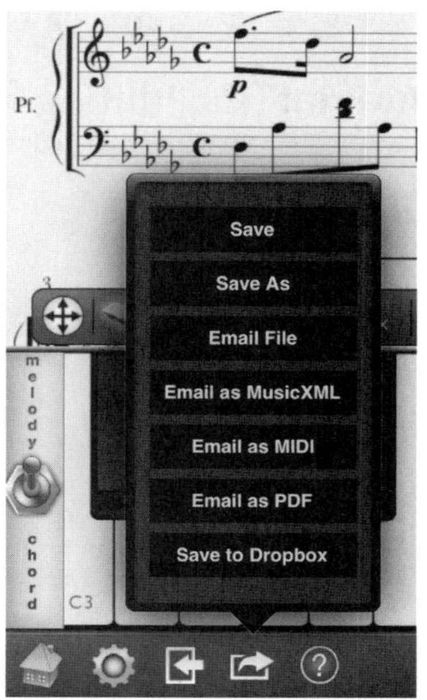

Figure 6.11. Notion saving options.

Sharing and Integrating with Common Desktop Notation Software

Finale 2012 and later and Sibelius 7 will both import and export MusicXML. So it is possible to work on a project on Notion, export the file in MusicXML, and then open it in Finale or Sibelius. You can go the other way as well, so you can take the file back into Notion and edit it from there.

Dropbox

Dropbox was introduced in chapter 2. It can be used as a cloud storage of your files for all of your apps, including Notation. You can share folders with friends, colleagues, and students. With Dropbox, you can share files only with specific people and include a password so others cannot access the files. This keeps the files personal. And they can be shared without placing them on the Internet where anyone can download them.

Printing

There are two options with regard to printing the music that you create on the iPad. You can print on an AirPrint-compatible printer, or you can export the file in PDF format and print it from a Mac or PC.

Printing from a Computer

If you don't have access to an AirPrint-compatible printer, then save the music notation in PDF format. Save the file in a cloud app such as Dropbox, or e-mail the file to yourself or the person who wants a hard copy. Open the file on a Mac or PC that is connected to a printer, and print the file.

Tip: If you don't have access to a printer, you could also e-mail the file to an office-supply store and pay for them to print it for you. All of the major companies have this service, including www.fedex.com, www.ups.com, and others.

AirPrint (for Printing from the iPad)

www.apple.com/support/ipad/assistant/airprint/

VIDEO 6.5. PRINTING.

Figure 6.12.
http://youtu.be/9r75m_VUr0E

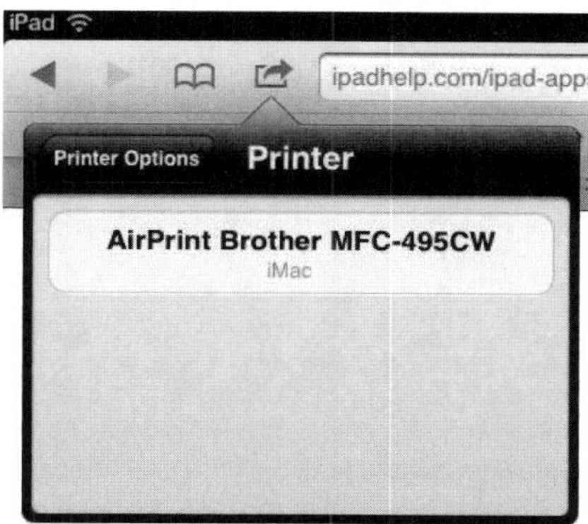

Figure 6.13. AirPrint.

Copyright Guidelines

When you are creating and sharing music notation files, be aware of the restrictions that are imposed by the copyright law.

What Is Copyright?

Legally, a copyright means that a musician, author, or artist has a "limited duration monopoly" on anything he or she creates. A work is automatically under copyright protection from the moment of creation: www.pdinfo.com/Copyright-Law/Copyright-Law.php.

Public Domain

There are works that are in the public domain. With music that was composed after 1978, copyright lasts for the life of the longest surviving author plus 70 years. So works by Mozart, Beethoven, and other composers are in public domain. If a piece is in public domain, it is not governed by copyright law. Be aware that an *arrangement* of a piece in public domain may be under copyright: http://musiced.nafme.org/resources/copyright-center/.

You can search for music that is in public domain at www.pdinfo.com.

Obtaining Permission to Use Copyrighted Music

It is possible to obtain permission to arrange and use copyrighted music. This is done by contacting the copyright owner. Check out the Music Publishers Association website for available forms and processes: www.mpa.org/content/copyright-resource-center.

Creative Commons Public License

You and others can give the public permission to modify and use specific works commercially. This is done via the Creative Commons category. A Creative Commons license is a public copyright license that allows for the distribution of copyrighted works. A Creative Commons license is used when an author wants to give the public the right to share, use, and even build upon a work that he or she has created: http://creativecommons.org/.

Fair Use

Educators have special dispensation with regard to copyright in education known as fair use. It is a bit complicated, but it allows teachers to use copyrighted works in specific situations: http://musiced.nafme.org/resources/copyright-center/copyright-law-what-music-teachers-need-to-know/.

The Bottom Line

If a piece of music is copyrighted, then ask permission before you enter it into your notation app or distribute it to others. Be sure that any use of a copyrighted work with students falls under fair use.

Chapter 6 Activities

1. Import a MIDI file into Notion.
2. Import a MusicXML file into Notion.
3. Search for free scores to download to Notion.
4. Create the melody, chords, and lyrics to "Aura Lee" in Notion.
5. Save "Aura Lee" in PDF format and send it to forScore (see chapter 4) for reading.
6. Save a Notion song in MIDI format and open it in GarageBand (see chapter 5).
7. Export a file from Notion in MusicXML format and import it into computer-based software Finale Notepad, Finale, or Sibelius.

Summary

This chapter focused on music notation applications that include creating and composing music using standard music notation. Understanding MIDI and MusicXML file formats is key when working with music notation. Several apps were reviewed for creating music notation. Saving files to the cloud and sharing them with others was covered. Being aware of copyright law and its restrictions is important when sharing and arranging music notation.

Chapter 7
LEARNING MUSIC

This chapter focuses on using apps to help you develop your musicianship skills, assist in learning to play an instrument, or further your knowledge of music history and related areas. The chapter is organized into four sections: musicianship skills, music history, learning an instrument, and practice tools.

Musicianship Skills

This section includes apps designed to help you understand music theory, from learning chords and scales to developing your musical ear.

Tenuto by musictheory.net ($3.99)

https://itunes.apple.com/us/app/tenuto/id459313476?mt=8

Tenuto includes 13 customizable exercises designed to enhance musicianship skills.

Figure 7.1. Tenuto.

The app comes from the popular music-theory website www.musictheory.net. There are staff-based and keyboard-based modules, including:

- Note Identification
- Key Signature Identification
- Interval Identification
- Chord Identification
- Keyboard Identification
- Keyboard Interval Identification
- Keyboard Chord Identification
- Fretboard Identification
- Interval Ear Training
- Scale Ear Training
- Chord Ear Training

This app is for students and musicians who want to brush up on certain aspects of music theory and/or ear training.

VIDEO 7.1. TENUTO DEMO.

Figure 7.2.
http://youtu.be/vfD0DsTccvw

> **Tip:** Some apps have web-based options where you can use them on a Mac or Windows computer. For example: www.musictheory.net.

Chords and Scales

If you play a chordal instrument such as the piano or guitar, there are some excellent apps to help you learn about and analyze chords.

Chord Lab by RoGame Software ($7.99)

http://ipad.rogame.com/pages/ChordLab.html

Chord Lab is designed for guitar players and can be used by performers, arrangers, and composers. It is a fairly advanced app with a focus on chord spelling and voice leading.

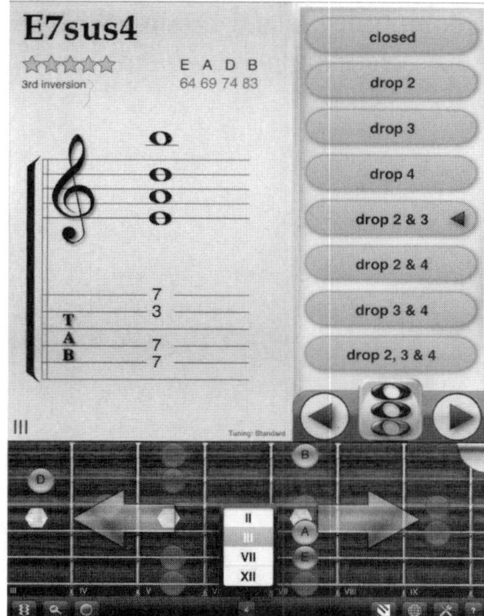

Figure 7.3. Chord Lab.

If you need to figure out the spelling of a specific chord or if you can play a chord but are not sure what to call it, this app can be extremely helpful. It will also show you the guitar fretboard for specific chords with suggested fingerings.

The guitar instrument includes a tunings window. All common standard and open tunings as well as a custom setting are available from the Tunings Picker at the top of the window. Strings can be tuned by seven semitones higher or lower than the standard tuning. Experimenting with tunings is a great way to find chord voicings that are not available in the standard tuning and thus expanding one's vocabulary.

VIDEO 7.2. CHORD LAB DEMO.

Figure 7.4.
http://vimeo.com/rogame/chordlabipad

ScaleMaster by RoGame Software ($4.99)

https://itunes.apple.com/us/app/id290752460?mt=8

Designed for the beginning musician as well as the professional, ScaleMaster is geared toward scale theory. You can quickly look up a scale, listen to it, or find out how to play it on an instrument. The app includes banjo, bass, guitar, mandolin, and piano instruments; alto, bass, tenor, and treble clefs; adjustable positions for all instruments; adjustable tuning for all string instruments; global transposition for horn players;

presets for common banjo, bass, guitar, and mandolin tunings; and support for five- and six-string bass. If you want to brush up on your scales and have a handy app to learn about new scales, then this app is for you.

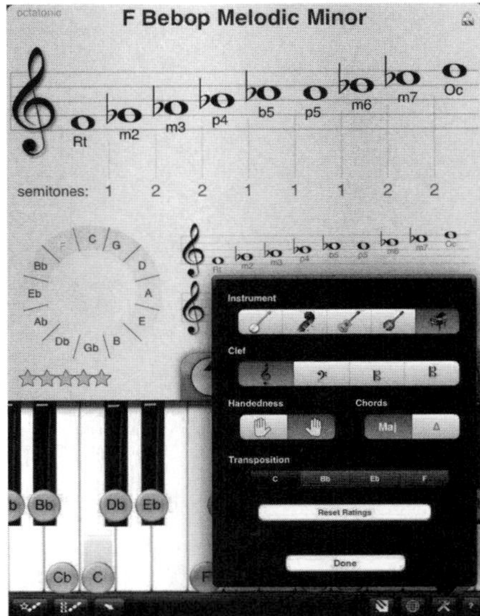

Figure 7.5. ScaleMaster.

VIDEO 7.3. SCALEMASTER DEMO.

Figure 7.6.
www.youtube.com/watch?v=-LDMIfJcpYc

Scale Tapper by Difint, LLC ($3.99)

https://itunes.apple.com/app/scale-tapper/id448231236?mt=8

This app is designed for any fretted instrument and helps you learn chords. You can easily select the chord you want to learn. You can search for chord names and substitutions using the Pitch Wizard, and all of the notation can be instantly converted to guitar tablature. Whether you play a balalaika or a 12-string guitar or anything in between, with Scale Tapper you have the power to tune and create your very own string instrument. You can visualize scales and chords and listen to them note by note, forward and backward, on the built-in music staff. You can invent some new chord fingerings on the tablature and jam on the interactive fretboard.

Figure 7.7. Scale Tapper.

VIDEO 7.4. SCALE TAPPER DEMO.

Figure 7.8.
www.youtube.com/watch?v=FuyLFv9RBPU

Ear Training

A trained ear is one of the most important skills a performer can develop.

Better Ears for iPad ($14.95)

https://itunes.apple.com/us/app/id364388065?mt=8&src=af&ign-mpt=uo%3D6

Karajan® Pro provides lessons that teach you to recognize intervals, chords, scales, pitch, and tempo with detailed statistics. It can display notation on a fretboard, piano keyboard, or music staff.

Figure 7.9. Karajan Pro.

This app is designed for the music hobbyist and music-theory students at the junior high, high school, or college level.

VIDEO 7.5. KARAJAN® PRO DEMO.

Figure 7.10.
https://www.youtube.com/watch?v=BRsFULdp-SY

EarMan by RoGame Software ($7.99)

https://itunes.apple.com/app/earman/id308737402?ign-mpt=uo%3D5

EarMan is designed for practicing intervals. It displays in standard music notation and includes a curriculum with 105 sessions from beginning to advanced interval recognition. It includes automatic grading of sessions. If you want to drill and practice intervals, this app is for you.

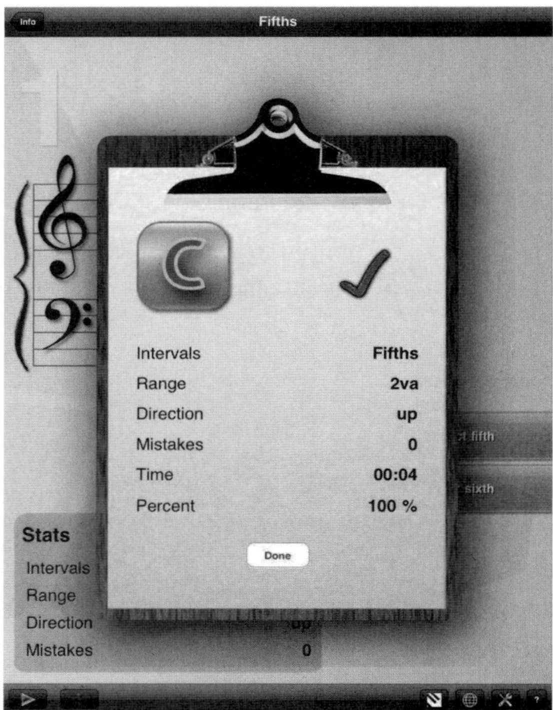

Figure 7.11. EarMan.

VIDEO 7.6. EARMAN DEMO.

Figure 7.12.
http://vimeo.com/rogame/earmanipad

Music History

Apps can be a wonderful way to learn about and explore the vast world of music history. They can turn a topic into an interactive experience and lead to heightened understanding and enjoyment.

History of Rock by ditter.projektagentur GmbH ($4.99)

https://itunes.apple.com/pl/app/history-of-rock/id468650707?mt=8

This comprehensive and well-illustrated history of rock music was compiled by renowned rock writer Mark Paytress. The app integrates YouTube videos and iTunes, making it possible to view featured musicians in action and sample song previews simply by clicking on the relevant icon.

The app guides you through rock music's first 60 years, a period that went through many remarkable changes as rock continued to draw on ever-wider influences, constantly reinventing itself.

From its origins in postwar America to its emergence as the siren call for the late-1960s youth revolution; from the theatrical, troubled 1970s to stadium rock and the digital age, rock music has proven to be remarkably resilient and adaptable—and remains more popular than ever. This app explains, in simple terms, how and why rock music has become such a potent force in popular culture.

Organized in roughly chronological fashion, the app's narrative is neatly divided into eras, each with its own key artists and rock-music styles. Breakout sections introduce relevant pop-culture fads and fashions, while an extensive timeline provides a continuous thread connecting all the elements that make up the story of rock music.

Figure 7.13. History of Rock.

VIDEO 7.7. HISTORY OF ROCK DEMO.

Figure 7.14.
https://www.youtube.com/watch?v=bu0vcIGt9A8

The History of Jazz— An Interactive Timeline by 955 Dreams ($9.99)

http://itunes.apple.com/us/app/history-jazz-interactive-timeline/id411521458?mt=8

If you are a fan of any type of jazz, this app will provide you with hours of entertainment. You can peruse the chronological history of jazz or learn about its seminal figures as each are presented with video and images. You can watch videos and read short biographies or dig deeper and read more thorough encyclopedic articles on each artist.

Included in the app is a list of essential jazz tunes and albums that allows you to sample each song and then decide if you want to include it in your own jazz collection with an integrated experience with iTunes (See chapter 1 for a demo of iTunes).

Figure 7.15. The History of Jazz.

VIDEO 7.8. THE HISTORY OF JAZZ DEMO.

Figure 7.16.
https://www.youtube.com/watch?v=cKphAh701Js

The Orchestra by Touch Press ($13.99)

https://itunes.apple.com/us/app/the-orchestra/id560078788?mt=8

Figure 7.17. The Orchestra.

The Orchestra is an extraordinary app that will delight all classical music lovers, from the novice to the expert.

Esa-Pekka Salonen conducts the world-renowned Philharmonia, performing extended extracts from eight works representing three centuries of symphonic music. The app allows real-time selection of multiple video and audio tracks, along with an automatically synchronized score and dynamic, graphical note-by-note visualization of each piece as it is played.

- Haydn: Symphony No. 6
- Beethoven: Symphony No. 5
- Berlioz: Symphony fantastique
- Debussy: Prélude à l'après midi d'un faune
- Mahler: Symphony No. 6
- Stravinsky: The Firebird
- Lutosławski: Concerto for Orchestra
- Salonen: Violin Concerto

The result is an immersive environment for exploring the music and all the instruments of the orchestra. It's helpful to listen to comments by the conductor and the introductions to all of the instruments.

VIDEO 7.9. THE ORCHESTRA DEMO.

Figure 7.18.
https://www.youtube.com/watch?v=QeenVPHSCe8

Learning an Instrument

Whether you already play a musical instrument or would like to learn how to play one, the iPad can be an excellent portable music tutor. Like the other applications mentioned in previous chapters, the major advantage to learning on your iPad is that the apps are relatively inexpensive (much more inexpensive than a live teacher!)

Learning Guitar

Guitar Lessons: Rock Prodigy by The Way of H Inc. ($29.99)

https://itunes.apple.com/app/guitar-lessons-rock-prodigy/id407303228?mt=8

Rock Prodigy offers a complete course on guitar that will help you learn foundational and practical music concepts. The comprehensive curriculum will assist you in what and how to practice and focus your ear on. The app will also track your progress. You need to own a guitar—electric or acoustic. This is a bit on the pricey side for apps, but you get a lot for the investment.

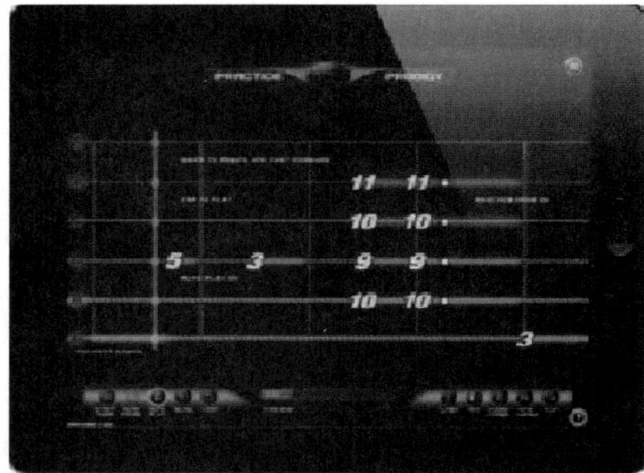

Figure 7.19.

VIDEO 7.10 GUITAR LESSONS DEMO.

Figure 7.20.
www.youtube.com/watch?v=M0BHbAsGgaI

GuitarToolkit by Agile Partners ($9.99)

https://itunes.apple.com/us/app/guitartoolkit/id284962368?mt=8

This is a suite of programs built into one. It supports any string instrument, including 6-, 7-, and 12-string guitar; 4-, 5-, and 6-string bass; banjo, mandolin, and ukulele—each with standard and alternate tunings. Tuner, chords, scales, and arpeggios automatically adapt for the selected instrument and tuning. The app has an excellent chromatic tuner similar to the one mentioned in chapter 1. There is a massive library of over two million chords, scales, and arpeggios for you to learn from. GuitarToolkit includes a chord finder that can answer the often-asked question "What chord is this?"

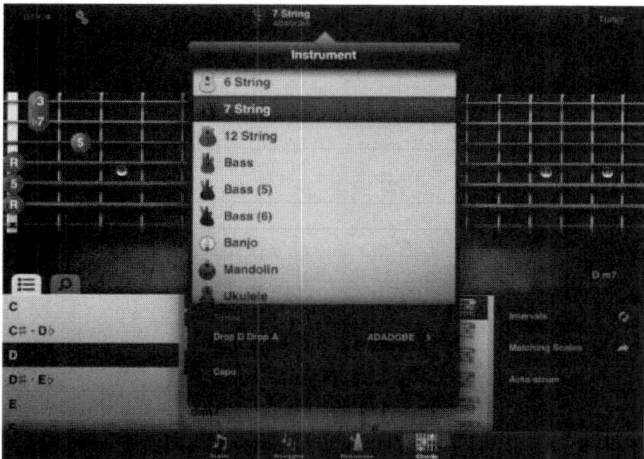

Figure 7.21.

VIDEO 7.11. GUITAR TOOLKIT DEMO.

Figure 7.22.
https://www.youtube.com/watch?v=1sGR4P9rPH0

> **Tip:** If you are using an instrument method, check to see if it supports an iPad app for practice. For example, Guitar Lab by TrueFire is a free app for students using the TrueFire online lessons. Also, www.pianowithwillie.com/ is a video-based lesson series that also offers a free iPad app with lessons.

Learning Piano

If you are currently a piano player or a wannabe, check out these apps to help you learn to play songs and improve your playing.

Nota by All Forces ($2.99)

https://itunes.apple.com/us/app/nota/id333179169?mt=8

For beginners, Nota's tools cover the basics of music notation, with a four-octave piano that displays the notes on a staff, along with a full-screen landscape-mode piano for practicing and an interactive-notes quiz to test your knowledge.

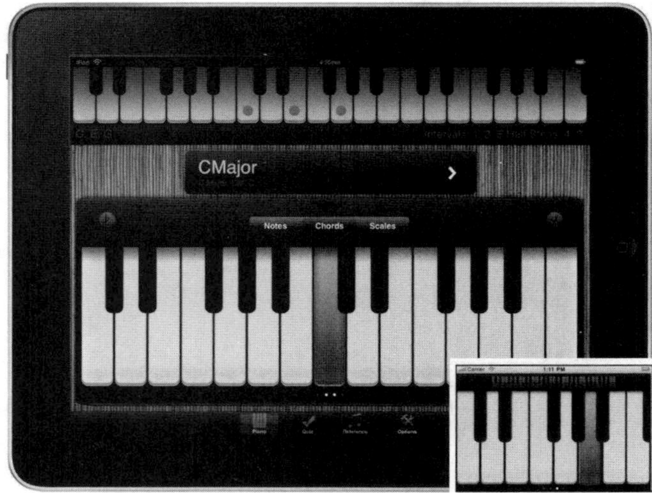

Figure 7.23.

For more experienced piano players, the scales browser has a comprehensive list of common and exotic scales. The app will show the scale, play it, and display the notes, intervals, and half steps. The chord's browser makes it easy to find a chord and play it on any key or invert it. You can also consult the Circle of Fifths in the reference section, which has a comprehensive reference of music notation.

VIDEO 7.12. NOTA DEMO.

Figure 7.24.
http://www.youtube.com/watch?v=exlQgRYOR-8

ezPiano for iPad: 100+ Songs with Full Accompaniment! by Eric Ching ($3.99)

https://itunes.apple.com/hk/app/ezpiano-for-ipad-100+-songs/id388546114?mt=8

ezPiano works like Guitar Hero for the piano. Whether you're a pro or an amateur, you'll find something cool to do with it. Unlike other piano apps, ezPiano shows you the sheet music and plays the accompaniment for you while you are playing the tune. Songs include Broadway, classical, and folk. There are several modes, including Song Mode, where you can set the app to play the song, or Learn Mode, where you can learn it yourself.

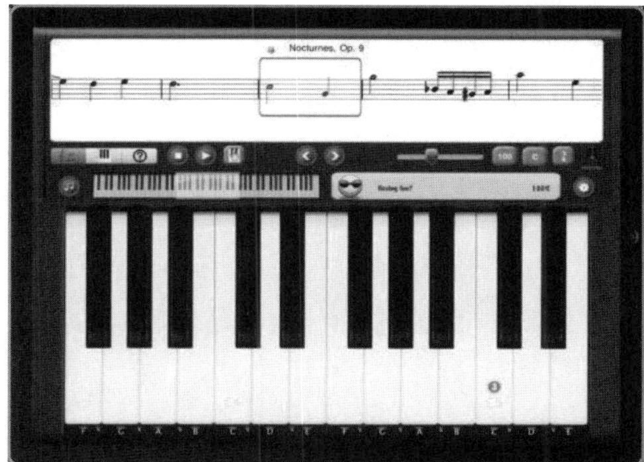

Figure 7.25.

VIDEO 7.13. EZPIANO DEMO.

Figure 7.26.
http://www.youtube.com/watch?v=eN8ZBGEUakw

Piano Lesson PianoMan for iPad by Yudo Inc. ($6.99)

https://itunes.apple.com/gb/app/piano-lesson-pianoman-for/id363724991?mt=8

This app is partly a tutorial and partly a game. You can learn to play 150 classical songs. Composers include Chopin, Beethoven, Mozart, Debussy, and others. The music is shown on the screen and prompts you to play the correct note. You can set the difficulty level so you can ease your way into becoming an expert classical pianist.

Figure 7.27.

VIDEO 7.14. PIANOMAN DEMO.

Figure 7.28.
www.youtube.com/watch?v=Wo97ZzuECCI

Brass Instrument Fingerings

There are apps for brass players that include fingering charts and other support material. These can be helpful to have by your side while playing or practicing a traditional brass instrument such as trumpet, French horn, or trombone.

Fingering Brass by Patrick Q. Kelly ($5.99)

https://itunes.apple.com/sg/app/fingering-brass/id367215632?mt=8

Need to look up the fingerings for a brass instrument? Fingering Brass provides fingering charts, which include alternate fingerings. Click on the staff or keyboard to display the proper fingering for trumpet. Includes fingerings for:

- French Horn: F, B♭ double; treble and bass clefs.
- Trumpets: A, B♭, C, and D; includes cornet and flugelhorn.
- Trombones: Tenorbass B♭, F, and bass B♭, F, G♭, D; treble, tenor, and bass clefs.
- Euphonium and Baritone: Treble, tenor, and bass clefs.
- Tubas: BB♭, CC, E♭, and F; treble and bass clefs.

Figure 7.29.

Woodwind Instruments

Fingering Woodwinds by Patrick Q. Kelly ($6.99)

https://itunes.apple.com/cy/app/fingering-woodwinds/id367215243?mt=8

Fingering Woodwinds offers over 1,200 fingerings, including many alternates for the following instruments:

- Flutes (Piccolo, Concert, Alto and Bass)—including m2, M2, m3, and M3 trill fingerings.
- Oboe and Cor Anglais—including m2 and M2 trill fingerings.
- Clarinets (Soprano, Alto, Bass and Contrabass)—including m2 and M2 trill fingerings.
- Bassoon and Contrabassoon—including m2 and M2 trill fingerings (treble, tenor, and bass clefs).
- Saxophones (Soprano, Alto, Tenor and Baritone)—including m2, M2, m3, and M3 trill fingerings.
- Alto and Tenor Sax—including altissimo fingerings up to written F, two octaves above the top-line F of the treble clef.

You pick a written note (by touching the staff), and then the woodwind fingering is displayed and the concert pitch played on the piano. Play a concert pitch on the piano, and the fingering is displayed and the transposed note written on the staff.

Fingering Woodwinds also includes a Piano mode that displays the note name, the location on the piano, and the notation in four different clefs: treble, alto, tenor and bass.

Figure 7.30.

VIDEO 7.15. FINGERING WOODWINDS.

Figure 7.31.
http://youtu.be/AQIK0N0vLt8

The String Family

Fingering Strings by Patrick Q. Kelly ($6.99)

https://itunes.apple.com/mg/app/fingering-strings/id413650899?mt=12

Fingering Strings is an app for violin, viola, cello, and double bass. Simply pick a written note (by clicking the staff), and the finger placements are displayed and concert pitch played on the piano. When you play a concert pitch on the piano, the finger placements are displayed and that pitch's note written on the staff.

Select to display each of the 15 positions for the violin and viola, 16 positions for the cello, and either 12 Simandl positions or 6 Rabbath positions on the double bass. The app displays the placement of "beginner tape" on the fingerboard for all the instruments, as well as string names and colors. You can view notation in treble, alto, tenor or bass clef.

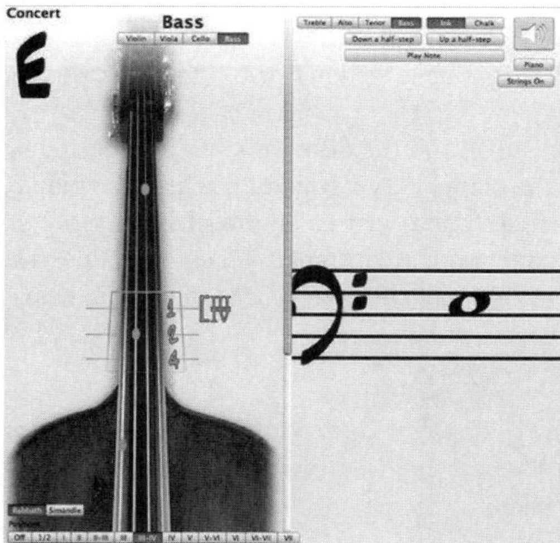

Figure 7.32.

Practice and Performance Tools

One of the most fun and productive apps you can purchase is one designed to enhance practice time with your instrument. There are apps designed specifically to help you develop your instrumental and/or vocal skills.

Tip: For music practice, headphones are helpful especially with apps that record what you are playing or singing via the iPad microphone. See chapter 1 for headphone information and options.

iReal b—Music Book & Play Along by Technimo LLC ($7.99)

https://itunes.apple.com/app/id298206806?mt=8&ign-mpt=uo%3D4

Company website: www.irealb.com/ios

This app is a music fake book and a live rhythm section. Well, it's not really live, but it will play back piano (or guitar), bass, and drums for any song when you simply type in the chord changes and choose a style. You can create, edit, print, and share chord charts of your favorite songs for reference while practicing or performing.

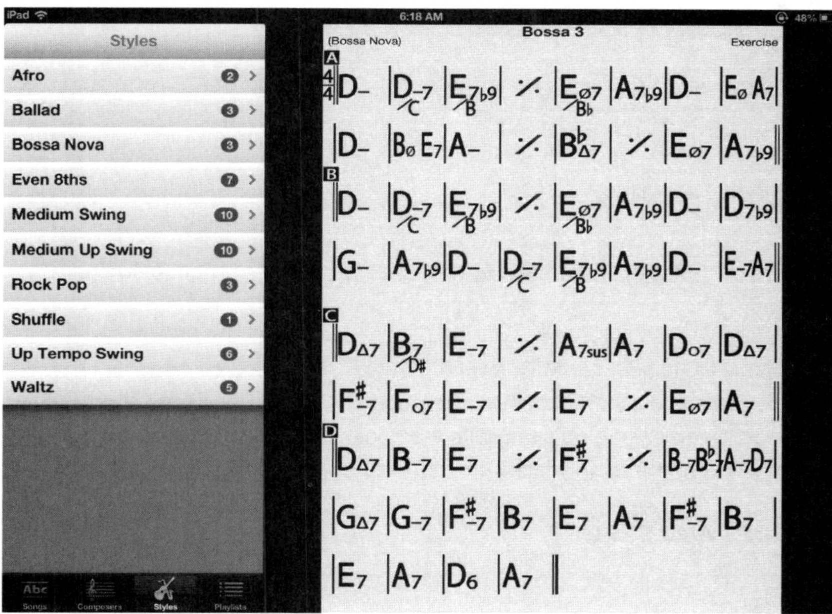

Figure 7.33.

In addition to the basic styles that come with the app, you can download additional styles for $5.99 each within the app.

iReal b comes with sample accompaniments. However, one of the major benefits of the app is the ability to enter the chords for any tune you want to practice. You can also download chords for many songs from the iReal b website right from the app.

Once you have imported or created the chord symbols for a desired tune, you can set the tempo, transpose it to any key, loop selected measures for specified practice with automatic tempo increase, and use automatic key transposition. The transpositions for horn players include E♭, B♭, F, and G. You can share individual charts or whole playlists with other iReal b users via e-mail and forums.

There are many extra app items that can be purchased for an additional fee. These include a host of style packs for jazz, Latin, and pop genres. These cost between $3.00 and $6.00. Many excellent features include chord scales ($2.99), where the scale for each chord symbol is displayed at the bottom of the screen during playback. Other add-on features include guitar chords, which display guitar chord diagrams during playback following the chord progression. Access the extensive chord diagrams library for quick and easy reference. Piano chords display piano chord diagrams during playback following the chord progression. You can also access the extensive chord diagrams library for quick and easy reference.

You can export chord charts as JPEG, PDF and MusicXML. MusicXML files can be read by iPad notation software (see chapter 6), as well as by computer-based notation software such as Finale and Sibelius. iReal b supports iRig, Amplitude, and other guitar connection kits, as well as AirTurn and other Bluetooth page turners.

VIDEO 7.16 IREAL B.

Figure 7.34.
www.youtube.com/watch?v=GpRcT9plDQg

Tip: If you want to record yourself playing with iReal b or other practice software, you can:

1. Export the practice file in audio or MIDI format.
2. Import the exported audio file into another app, such as GarageBand (see chapter 5).
3. Record yourself playing or singing along with the audio track. Headphones should be used so the iPad microphone only picks up your instrument or voice.

VIDEO 7.17 IMPORT AND EXPORT.

Figure 7.35.
http://youtu.be/K5GpU-_so9E

BandMaster HD by RoGame Software ($7.99)

https://itunes.apple.com/lk/app/bandmaster-hd/id369950819?mt=8

Company site: http://ipad.rogame.com/pages/BandMaster.html
BandMaster is a similar app to iReal b, above. It has many of the same features. The look and feel of the app is a bit more pleasing, but the features are not as expansive as iReal b's.

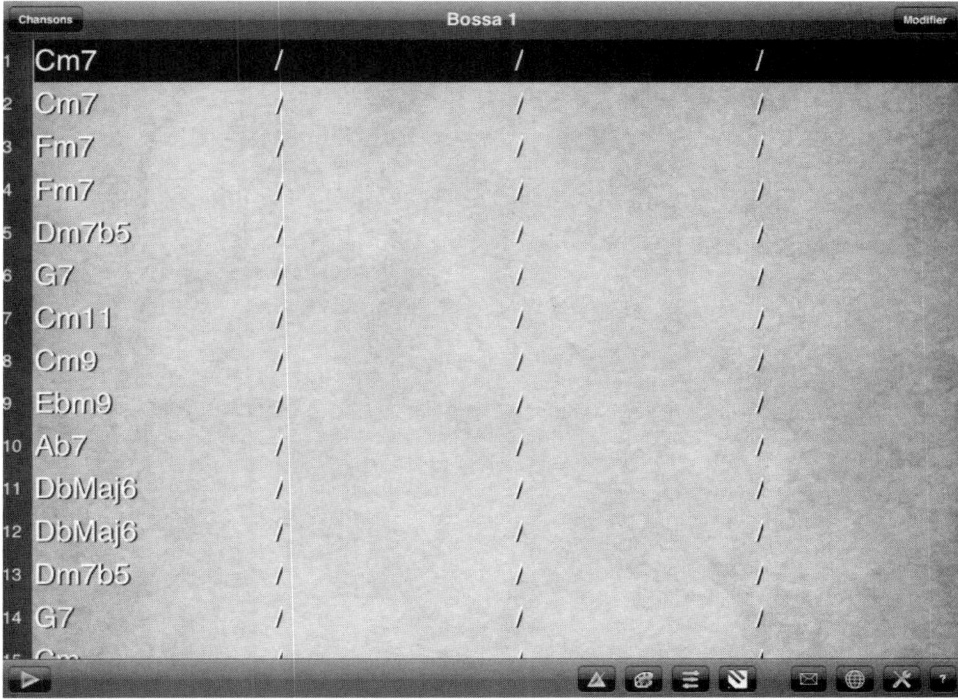

Figure 7.36.

The playback view displays the chords in a grid that scrolls down and highlights each measure as it is played. You determine the speed and number of choruses as well as the style. If you like, you can also turn off any of the instruments. You can even have your band's logo as the background for the playback view.

You can create new songs with one of the many templates available. Other templates include exercises and blues, as well as jazz-standard forms of different lengths.

The current version only supports exchanging songs via the Mac OS app, which is a separate purchase for $24.99.

VIDEO 7.18. BANDMASTER DEMO.

Figure 7.37.
http://vimeo.com/77436321

SmartMusic for iPad
(Free/Subscription to Access Library of Music: $40.00)

www.smartmusic.com

SmartMusic is a practice and play-along software tool. The one difference with this app is that you can't create your own chords or songs unless you own a full version of the computer-based Notation software Finale, available for Mac and Windows. And if you want to access the thousands of songs and pieces, it requires an annual subscription, which is currently $40 per year. An amazing amount of music from every genre is available. Included are all wind and string instruments and voice (no guitar or piano).

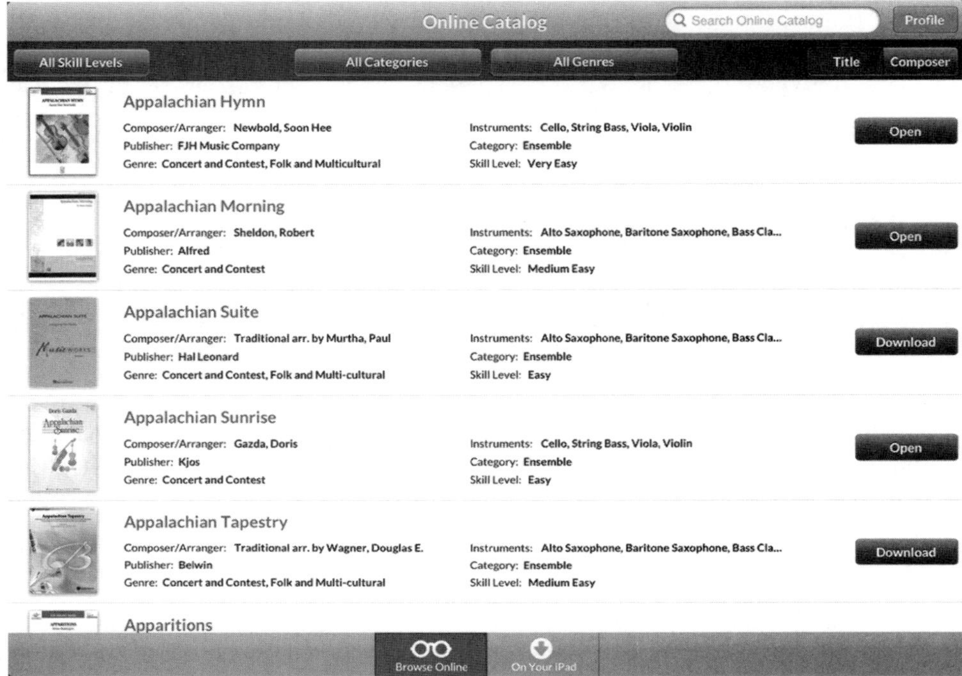

Figure 7.38.

Once you have purchased a subscription, you can use SmartMusic on your computer or the iPad app, just not at the same time. The music scrolls on the screen.

The feedback is outstanding. It indicates correct and incorrect notes and provides fingerings for all instruments. It is certainly worth the annual subscription cost.

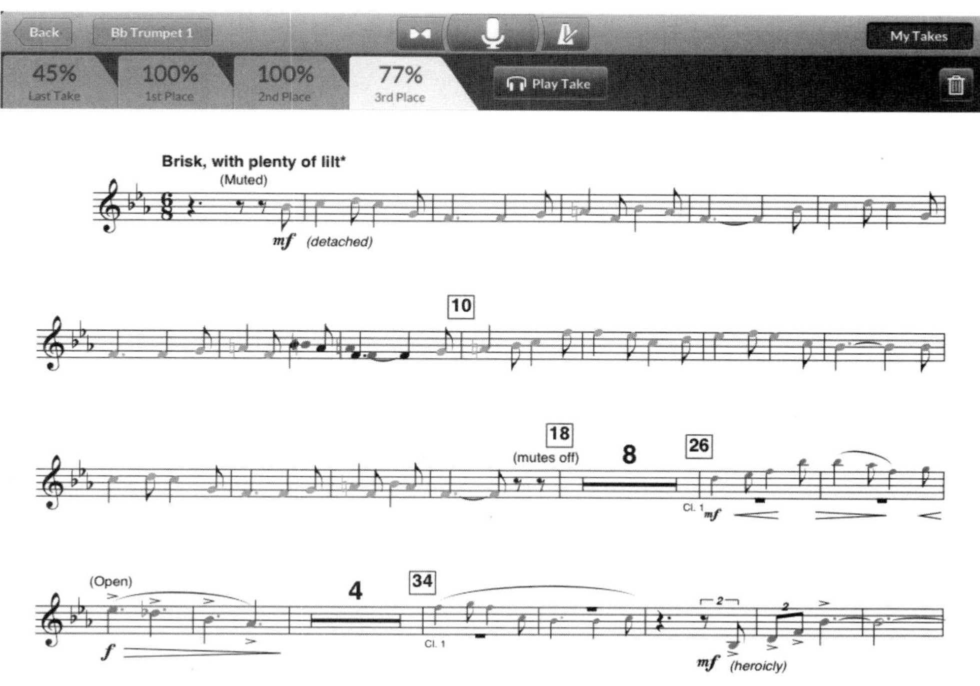

Figure 7.39.

VIDEO 7.19. SMARTMUSIC DEMO.

Figure 7.40.
http://youtu.be/0_NYP8xcxdQ

Brass Practice Apps by Contact Plus Corporation ($4.99)

- Trumpet Pro HD: https://itunes.apple.com/mt/app/trumpet-pro-hd/id373849878?mt=8.
- Trombone Pro HD: https://itunes.apple.com/hk/app/trombone-pro-hd/id392305654?mt=8.
- French Horn Pro HD: https://itunes.apple.com/us/app/french-horn-hd/id374207811?mt=8.

These brass instrument apps are specifically designed to allow you to actually play the fingerings or trombone positions on the iPad to generate a realistic fingering and aural practice tool. Designed for those who already know how to play the instrument, the apps help you practice with built-in exercises that include basic scales and many more.

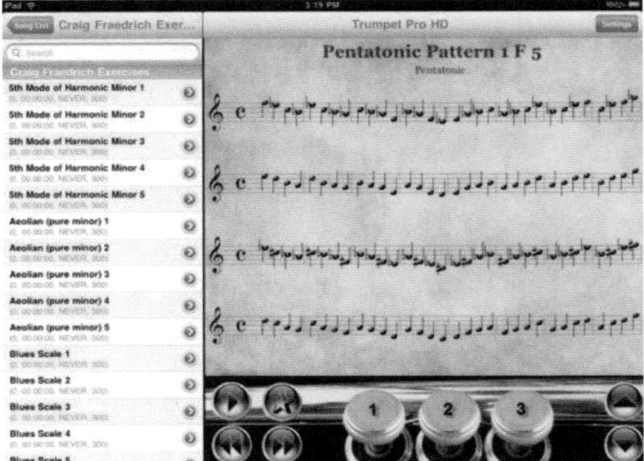

Figure 7.41.

You can edit each exercise and include piano chords for ear training, as well as view the name and possible fingering/slide positions for each note. In-app purchases are available, such as Bobby Shew's *Exercises and Etudes* book.

VIDEO 7.20. TRUMPET PRO HD DEMO

Figure 7.42.
www.youtube.com/watch?feature=player_embedded&v=u2ztRTVrqm8

Vocals

Singing Vocal Warm Ups—
Singer's Friend by Robert Lumpkins ($3.99)

https://itunes.apple.com/US/app/id350913803?mt=8&ign-mpt=uo%3D4

Have you ever found yourself in a situation where you could not find a piano to warm up with before a performance? Well, now your iPad can serve this purpose. With Singing Vocal Warm Ups, you choose the vocal range, scale pattern, and how fast the notes play. Singer's Friend then plays the scale pattern from the bottom of the selected range to the top and then back down again. Singer's Friend is perfect for singers of all levels and styles. Use it anytime to warm up for a performance, develop agility, or work on technique.

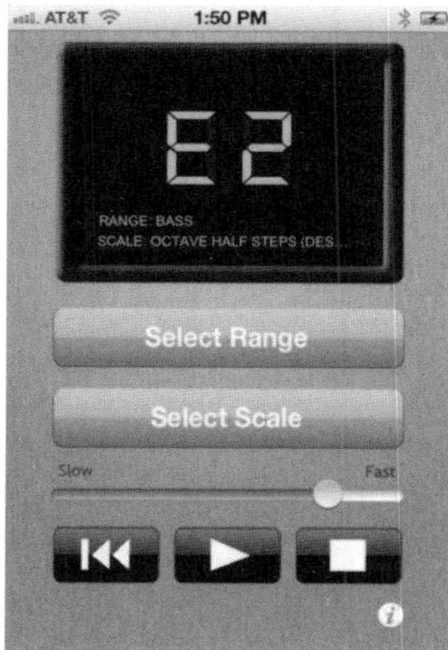

Figure 7.43.

Sing Harmonies by Zanna Discs ($2.99)

https://itunes.apple.com/US/app/id378913608?mt=8&ign-mpt=uo%3D4

Practice singing harmony and polish your vocal harmonizing skills. Each tune is presented so you can play or mute any of the vocal parts. Songs include:

- "Lean on Me"
- "Teach Your Children"
- "Proud Mary"

All of the vocals are presented aurally, so there is no need to read music notation.

Figure 7.44.

Sing! Karaoke by Smule (Free)

https://itunes.apple.com/us/app/sing!-karaoke-by-smule/id509993510?mt=8

Sing! Karaoke is designed for your to use to sing your favorite songs from a huge catalog of songs from which to choose. After you record your version, you can choose to share it with the world using this app.

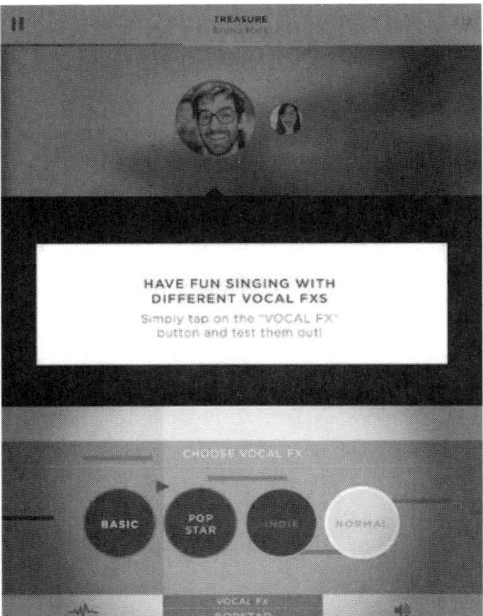

Figure 7.45.

VIDEO 7.21. SING! KARAOKE DEMO.

Figure 7.46.
http://youtu.be/4ax1gMhKvMo

Chapter 7 Activities

1. Compare the Tenuto app with its web counterpart: www.musictheory.net.
2. Using one of the music history apps, research a performer, composition, or event.
3. Enter the chords to a song in iReal b or BandMaster.
4. Export a file in MIDI format and import it into an audio program reviewed in chapter 5.
5. Export a chord chart in PDF format and send it to forScore or other software reviewed in chapter 4.
6. Using one of the music practice apps, practice playing or singing a song.
7. Export the song in audio format, and use it in another music app of your choice.

Summary

There are many apps to enhance the learning and practicing of an instrument or voice. These include apps to help you learn music theory and sharpen your musical ear. Tutorial apps can provide you with a virtual teacher and give you feedback on your performance. Practice has never been more fun than with apps that provide you with a rhythm section . . . and much more.

Chapter 8
Music Education

This chapter focuses on iPad apps for music students and music educators. It explores how teachers can use the iPad for class presentations or to facilitate ensemble rehearsals. It reviews the myriad of ways that students can use the iPad in the music curriculum. Many of the apps reviewed in chapters 2 and 7 can be applied to aspects of music education. However, this chapter focuses on the apps that are specifically designed for young students or for use in the music classroom.

Presentation Tool

The iPad makes a fantastic presentation tool. There are some advantages to using an iPad to make a presentation compared to a Mac or Windows computer. The iPad is portable. A teacher can walk around the classroom or a rehearsal with the iPad easily in hand. The small size of the iPad makes it easy to place on a music stand or podium. Your fingers control the iPad, so there is no need to use a computer keyboard or mouse.

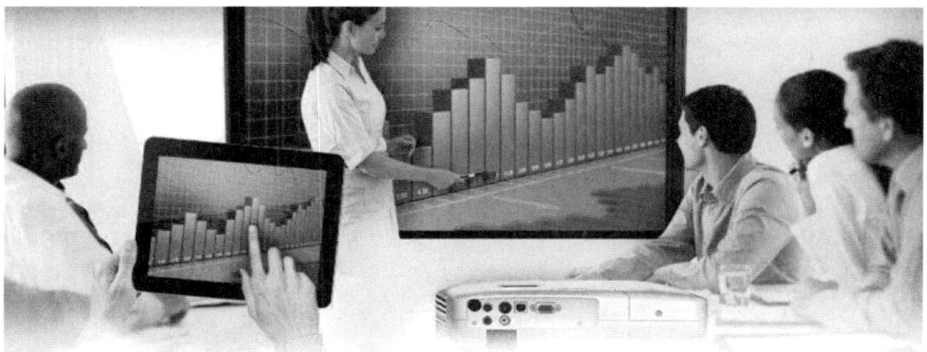

Figure 8.1. Projecting the iPad.

Projecting the iPad Screen

There are several ways to project the iPad screen so a class or group of students can see it. Most classrooms have either a computer projector or an interactive whiteboard for group display. If this is the case, then there are several ways to connect the output of the iPad so it can be projected for a group presentation or class.

Connecting to a Monitor via VGA Cable

One option is to connect your iPad to the projector using a VGA cable. You will need to have a VGA adapter that connects to your iPad and to the projector's VGA output, such as the Apple 30-pin to VGA adapter ($29.95) or Lightning to VGA adapter ($49.95).

Figure 8.2. iPad VGA connector.

The VGA connector is relatively inexpensive, and most projectors have a VGA input. The downside to a VGA connector is that you lose the mobility of the iPad, as you are tethered to the projector via the VGA cable. Granted, you could purchase a long VGA cable, but this option is best when the presenter is stationary in the front of the room or behind a podium.

Connect via Apple TV

Apple TV is a wireless device made by Apple. It allows you to connect wirelessly to display devices such as HD TV and other projection devices, and it lists for $99. You can connect a computer projector to an Apple TV via the high-definition multimedia interface (HDMI) connector. Then you can wirelessly connect the iPad. Once the iPad is connected, the iPad screen is displayed on the computer projector.

> **Tip:** If the projector does not support HDMI, then you can purchase an adapter such as the Kanex ATVPRO AirPlay Mirroring for VGA Projector, which lists for $59, and use that to connect your Apple TV to the projector: www.kanexlive.com/atvpro.

The advantage of Apple TV is that the iPad is not physically connected to the unit, so the presenter can walk around the room while presenting.

VIDEO 8.1. CONNECTING VIA APPLE TV.

Figure 8.3.
http://youtu.be/VDfsbdKfQyk

Connect via AirServer

With AirServer software, www.airserver.com, you can wirelessly connect your iPad display to your Mac or PC and from there to your projector, SmartBoard or HDTV. The cost is $14.99 for a standard license and $11.99 for a student license.

Figure 8.4. Airserver software.

If you can connect your Mac or PC computer to a projector, you can then use AirServer to connect wirelessly to your iPad and display the iPad screen on the projector. The iPad's display is now on the computer screen, and the computer can project it to the classroom screen. This is a very inexpensive way to connect the iPad to a projector or other device. Although inexpensive, the process has a few steps. You must install AirServer and then connect it to the computer wirelessly. It's definitely not rocket science, but it does take more time than simply plugging in a VGA cable.

Tip: The videos that were created for this book used AirServer so we could capture the iPad display.

AirServer also supports multiple simultaneous connections, so one or more students could mirror their iPads to share their ideas and their work with the rest of the class at the same time.

Presentation Software

Now that you have a way to display the iPad to a large audience via a computer projector or interactive whiteboard, you will need a way to create your presentations.

Pointer by Karmeye (Free)

https://itunes.apple.com/us/app/pointer/id424823677?mt=8

VIDEO 8.2 POINTER SOFTWARE.

Figure 8.5.
www.youtube.com/watch?v=IlJQ1r0hCbg

> **Tip:** With apps, in most cases, "free" is not entirely free. The free apps typically have a cost factor to them. For example, the above app, Pointer, is free so long as you only want to use it with files you can access directly from specific websites or locations. If you want to open files from cloud options such as Dropbox, you have to make an in-app purchase.

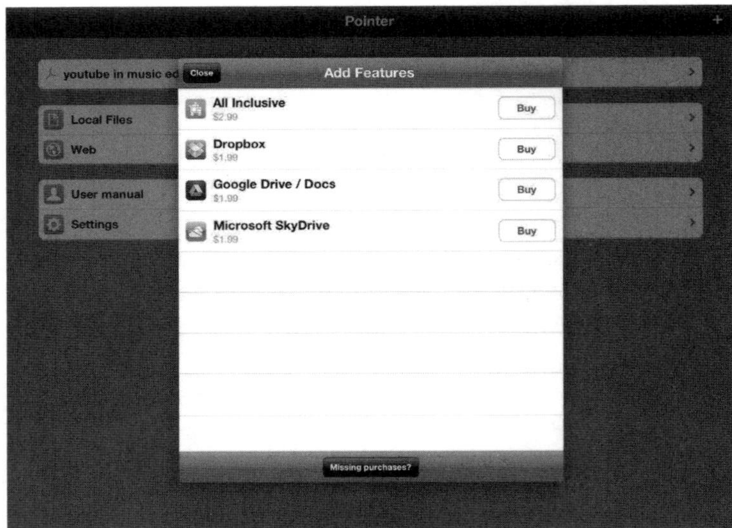

Figure 8.6. Pointer added features.

Keynote by Apple ($9.99)

https://itunes.apple.com/us/app/keynote/id361285480?mt=8

Apple's Keynote was originally created for the Mac, and now there is a powerful version for the iPad. Keynote was designed by the late cofounder of Apple, Steve Jobs, and used in his legendary annual presentations.

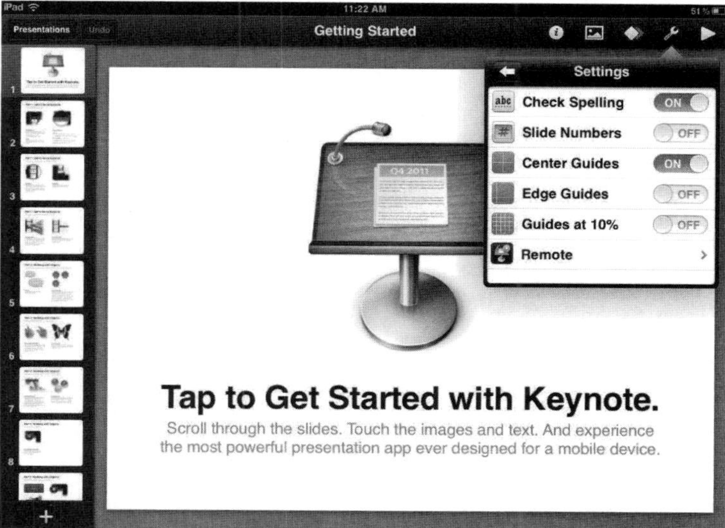

Figure 8.7. Keynote by Apple.

Keynote for iPhone and iPad is simply an amazing tool for creating, sharing, and editing presentations. It is a one-stop app, and it is extremely powerful. There are many excellent tutorials available on the Internet on how to use this popular app. It is worth the time and effort to learn, because you can create scintillating presentations on your iPad. They are stored on iCloud, so you can access them from any of your devices. You can create your own presentations on the iPad or open Keynote presentations that you've created on your Mac computer.

Tip: You can control Keynote using your iPhone.

Keynote Remote by Apple ($0.99)

https://itunes.apple.com/US/app/id300719251?mt=8&ign-mpt=uo%3D4

To begin using the Keynote app on the iPad, select the Tools icon at the top right of the screen. Next, select Settings, and then Remote. Select your iPhone by clicking "Link." From there, type in the four-digit passcode you received on your handheld. Now you may control your iPad Keynote presentation using your iPhone. This app can also be used to control your Keynote presentations on your Mac computer.

PowerPoint Files

SlideShark: View & Share Presentations by Brainshark Inc. (Free)

https://itunes.apple.com/us/app/slideshark-powerpoint-presentations/id471369684?ls=1&mt=8

You likely have a lot of presentations already created on your Mac or PC using Microsoft PowerPoint. If this is the case, then the free app SlideShark is perfect for you. Once you download the app, you can upload a PowerPoint file from your computer, iPhone, or iPod touch. Supported file formats include PPT, PPTX, PPS, and PPSX. The app is free, but the company charges for additional storage space. You get 100 MB of storage for free. You can upgrade to 500 MB for $49, or 1 GB for $95 for an entire year.

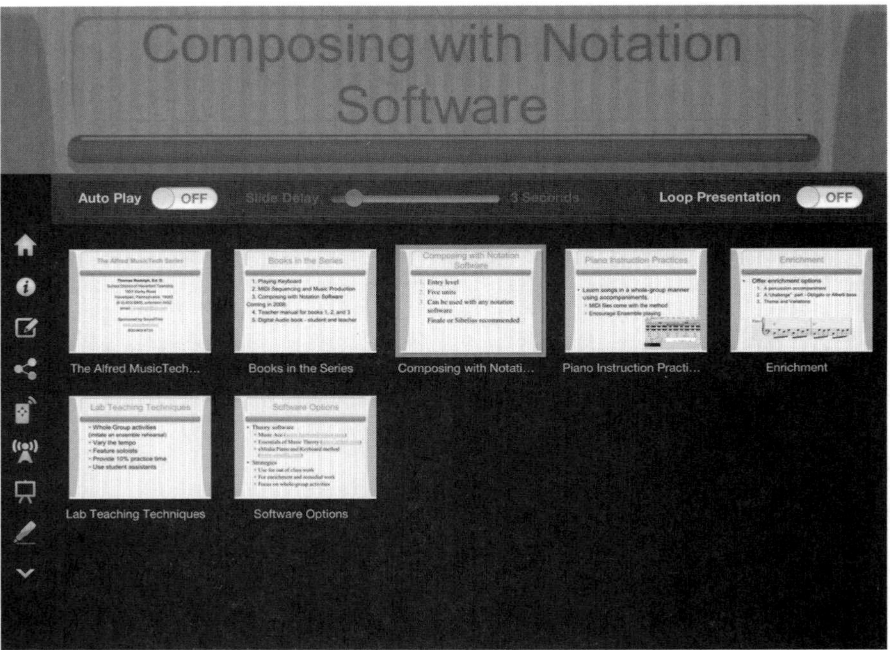

Figure 8.8. SlideShark.

In addition to downloading the app, you must set up an account at www.slideshark.com. Then you can upload your PowerPoint presentations. You can download and use SlideShark to present your PowerPoint presentations from any compatible device.

SlideShark's handy features include a light pen and drawing options. You can also broadcast your presentations over the Web in real time to multiple students, no matter what devices they are using.

You can't do a lot of editing in SlideShark, which is one of the few downsides to the application. That will need to be done on the computer using PowerPoint, which can then be uploaded to the SlideShark cloud storage.

VIDEO 8.3. SLIDESHARK.

Figure 8.9.
http://youtu.be/Hsq6veySMFw

Tip: You can take a screenshot of the iPad without installing any app. When you have the image you want to copy on the iPad screen:

1. Press and hold the Menu button (the main button below the screen).
2. With the Menu button held down, press the Power/Lock button (the switch on the top edge of the device).
3. Open the camera on your iPad, and the screen you just captured will be in your camera roll. Open it, and you can e-mail to yourself or others.

Google Drive by Google, Inc. (Free)

https://itunes.apple.com/us/app/google-drive/id507874739

Google Drive

One of the most popular cloud storage options for teachers and students is Google Drive and GoogleDocs. For an overview of this service, go to http://en.wikipedia.org/wiki/Google_Drive.

Using your iPad and Google Drive, you can access all of the files in your GoogleDrive. You can upload PDF files, PowerPoint files, and just about any file you want to use for group demonstration. When you launch Google Drive and enter your GoogleDrive username and password, you can access all of your files right from your iPad. The current version allows you to open GoogleDrive documents and share and edit them on your iPad.

VIDEO 8.4. GOOGLE DRIVE DEMO

Figure 8.10.
http://youtu.be/I7m7R3xI5GY

Teaching Tools

Whether you are teaching a private lesson or an ensemble such as a band, orchestra, or chorus, you can use apps to support your teaching. For example, the tuner and metronome apps mentioned in chapter 2 can be handy tools. Also, practice software such as iReal b (see chapter 7) can be an enhancement in the rehearsal. There are other tools to be considered designed specifically for teachers.

A.P.S. MusicMaster Pro by C. L. Barnhouse Company ($6.99)

http://itunes.apple.com/us/app/a.p.s.-musicmaster-pro/id441595661?mt=8

A.P.S. Music Master Pro is described as the "all in one" musicians' tool, with a variety of applications in the app. Music Master Pro includes a PDF viewer and annotator; chromatic tuner with pitch pipe, audio recorder, and player; metronome; timer/stopwatch; instrumental/vocal ranges and transpositions; common guitar chords; fingering charts; and musical terms and translations.

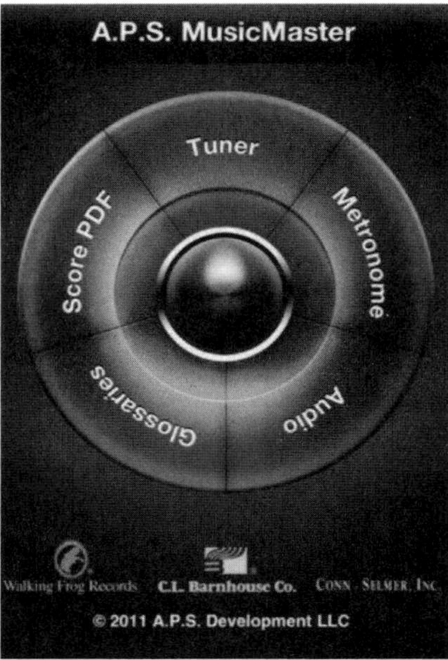

Figure 8.11. A.P.S. Music Master Pro.

Being able to access so many functions in one app is appealing. The PDF viewer includes an animator, so you can create custom-made presentation files for your students and audiences. Marking a score or part for analysis and demonstration is a snap.

The included tuner, audio recorder, and metronome can replace several apps, such as those mentioned in chapters 2 and 7. Music Master Pro also offers fingering charts and musical terms. This app can be a cornerstone for the teacher, student, or performer.

VIDEO 8.5. A.P.S. MUSIC MASTER PRO.

Figure 8.12. A.P.S. Music Master Pro.
http://youtu.be/0_NYP8xcxdQ

iBooks by Apple (Free)

https://itunes.apple.com/us/app/ibooks/id364709193?mt=8

iBooks was mentioned in chapter 4 as a way to organize PDF files of sheet music and more. It also is a platform where you can search for textbooks to read on the iPad. The app offers a full-screen experience full of interactive diagrams, photos, and videos.

With iBooks, students are not limited to text and pictures. They can experience interactive captions, rotate a 3D object, or have the answer appear in a chapter review. They can flip through a book by simply sliding a finger along the bottom of the screen. Highlighting text, taking notes, searching for content, and finding definitions in the glossary are just as easy. With all their books on a single iPad, students will have no problem carrying them wherever they go.

Figure 8.13. iBooks Music History search results.

With the free iBook app, searching through the thousands of books can yield some excellent texts for use in the music curriculum and to further your knowledge in a specific area. Many books are free, and some can be purchased.

iBooks Author by Apple (Requires a Mac Computer) (Free)

https://itunes.apple.com/us/app/ibooks-author/id490152466?mt=12

Figure 8.14. iBooks Author.

With iBooks Author, you can create and author textbooks for iPad using a Mac computer. Start with one of the Apple-designed templates that feature a wide variety of page layouts. Add your own text and images with drag-and-drop ease. Use multitouch widgets to include interactive photo galleries, movies, Keynote presentations, 3D objects, and more. Preview your book on your iPad at any time. You can then make your books available to students. There is an excellent help section on the Apple website: www.apple.com/support/ibooksauthor/.

iTunes U by Apple (Free)

https://itunes.apple.com/us/app/itunes-u/id490217893?mt=8

Apple iTunes was described in chapter 1. The app can also be an effective tool in the classroom for playing audio and video examples for students. Teachers can organize iTunes playlists for specific use, such as by class or ensemble. Then you will both have access to your library and have it organized in a way that will make your presentations more efficient.

Apple's iTunes U app makes available a vast library of content, including textbooks, videos, web links, and more within a single app. Install the app, and start browsing courses for your own review or for use with your students. You can access the world's largest online catalog of free education content from leading institutions such as Stanford, Yale, MIT, Oxford, and UC Berkeley, along with other institutions such as the Museum of Modern Art, the New York Public Library, and many more.

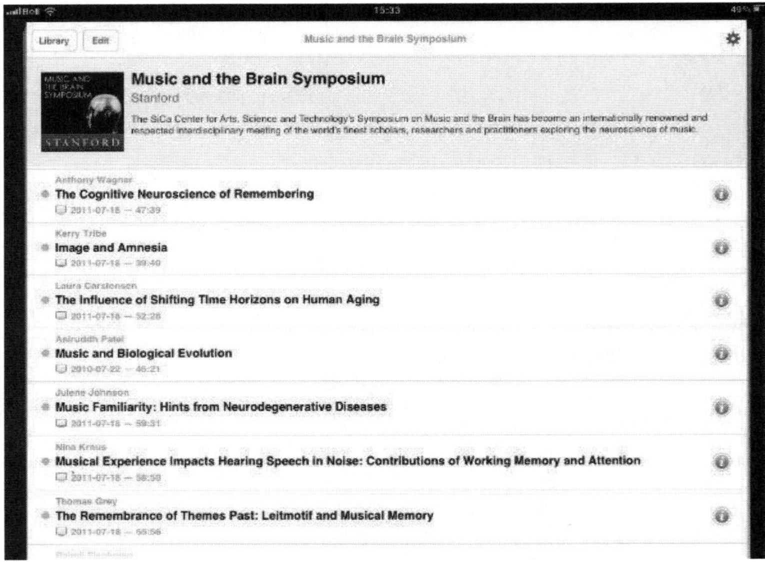

Figure 8.15. iTunes U.

From the iTunes U app, students can play video or audio lectures and take notes synchronized with the lecture. They can also read books and view presentations.

iTunes U Course Manager

Teachers can create courses that contain dynamic content including text, videos, and links, all via the iTunes U Course Manager. Signing up is free, and the course manager is web based, so you can access it from your Mac or PC or your iPad. To begin using iTunes U Course Manager to develop your own courses for your students:

1. Make sure you have a valid Apple ID.
2. Using your web browser, navigate to the iTunes U Course Manager portal: https://itunesu.itunes.apple.com/coursemanager/.
3. Sign in using your Apple ID username and password. If you don't have an Apple ID, you can create one by clicking on "create one now" from the login page.
4. Once you have signed in, you can begin creating courses.

Once your courses are on iTunes U, students can view them on any device: their iPad, Mac or PC computer, or any other device that can display a webpage. The iTunes U Students' site provides registered students with audio and video content taken from the modules they are studying. It provides a fast and easy-to-use alternative platform from which to access course content for any subject.

Tip: You can view several webcasts on the Apple site with a description of iTunes U and Course Manager: https://edseminars.apple.com/itunesu_webcast_series/. There are also many outstanding support websites available on the use of this powerful app, including http://deimos.apple.com/rsrc/doc/AppleEducation-iTunesUUsersGuide/Introduction/chapter_1_section_1.html.

VIDEO 8.6. ITUNES U OVERVIEW.

Figure 8.15a.
http://vimeo.com/59346698

Apps for Students

Many of the apps for music learning mentioned in chapter 7 can be used by students to drill and explore music theory and music history and with instrumental instruction. In addition, they can utilize the tuner and metronome apps mentioned in chapter 2. This section focuses on apps designed specifically for students.

Tip: There are some excellent websites and blogs to review for lists of apps that music teachers recommend. See the end of this chapter for a list of some of the teacher-resource webpages and blogs for continued support.

Music for Little Mozarts by Alfred Music Publishing ($0.99)

https://itunes.apple.com/us/app/music-for-little-mozarts/id412230593?mt=8&ign-mpt=uo%3D2

The Music for Little Mozarts piano app was specifically developed for preschool ages (four-, five-, and six-year-olds). The games provide a balance between learning key aspects of the piano and the pure enjoyment of making music. Students take an adventure with "Beethoven Bear" and "Mozart Mouse" as they learn about music.

Figure 8.16. Music for Little Mozarts.

AtPlayMusic Recorder by AtPlayMusic ($3.99)

http://itunes.apple.com/us/app/atplaymusic-recorder/id527965342?mt=8

In this app, students play their own recorder along with Mr. Noteworthy and an avatar classmate. It includes excellent tutorial and audio feedback for students. In-app purchases enable students to use fingering charts to learn additional tunes, including fun Christmas classics.

Figure 8.17. AtPlayMusic Recorder.

VIDEO 8.7. ATPLAYMUSIC RECORDER.

Figure 8.18.
http://www.youtube.com/watch?v=jV6i624Mww4&feature=share&list=UUexXbBSshXQnMB8C7klsBgg

4Music Rooms by TopCreations ($2.99)

https://itunes.apple.com/us/app/4-music-rooms/id443919368?mt=8

An educational music game for children, this app features four rooms that are used to organize activities that include learning the names of the piano keys, lines, and spaces of the staff, and note naming on the staff. The additional rooms help users learn rhythms and meter.

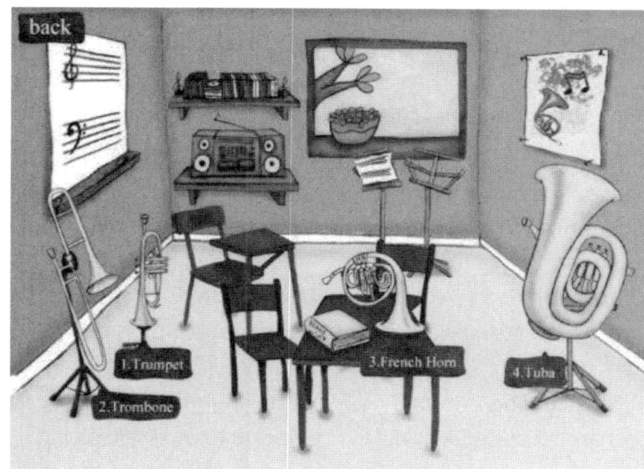

Figure 8.19. 4MusicRooms.

Tip: SmartMusic was described in lesson 7 but bears repeating here, as there are dozens of beginning band and string-instrument methods included with the annual subscription of $40. The app itself is free.

Music Technology in the Curriculum

Using iPad apps such as GarageBand and any of the other composition apps mentioned in chapters 5 and 6, students can record themselves, compose and create original music, and arrange and rearrange existing music.

There are some excellent books on using technology in the music curriculum that focus on composition. These books offer many ideas for ways to use technology in music education with specific examples for teachers. They are written by practicing music teachers.

- Making Music with GarageBand and Mixcraft by James Frankel, Michael Fein, Robin Hodson, and Richard McCready
  www.courseptr.com/Courses.aspx?q=garageband+and+mixcraft&x=0&y=0
- Teaching Music Through Composition by Barbara Freedman
  http://www.amazon.com/Teaching-Music-Through-Composition-Curriculum/dp/019984061X
- Teaching Music with Technology by Tom Rudolph
  www.giamusic.com/search_details.cfm?title_id=5639
- Technology Integration in the Elementary Music Classroom by Amy Burns
  www.halleonard.com/product/viewproduct.do?itemid=331764&lid=0&keywords=technology%20integration&subsiteid=1&
- Using Technology to Unlock Musical Creativity by Scott Watson
  http://www.amazon.com/Technology-Unlock-Musical-Creativity-ebook/dp/B005FVPG5S/

Education Support

There are a host of support groups and blogs in the area of music technology and education. Music teachers can join groups that focus on the integration of technology in music education. These include:

- TI:ME Technology in Music Education (www.ti-me.org/): There is a lot of free information on the website, and for an annual membership fee of $50, you can access special member areas of the website with hundreds of lesson plans, articles, and more.
- Association for Technology in Music Instruction (ATMI) (http://atmionline.org/): You can join their discussion e-mail group for free. Membership includes the registration fee to the annual conference.
- Mustech.net (Hosted by Dr. Joe Pisano): This site and its Facebook page (www.facebook.com/mustech.net) are an excellent way to connect with other music educators who are using technology in their teaching. There is an excellent post about iPads that has a host of comments from educators: www.mustech.net/2012/10/the-ipad-in-the-music-classroom-useful-tool-or-expensive-toy/.
- iPad and Technology in Music Education (Another Blog Hosted by Paul Simmons) (http://ipadmusiced.wordpress.com/): Includes excellent posts and responses from teachers.
- Teaching Music with Technology (www.linkedin.com/groups?gid=4148331&mostPopular=&trk=tyah): A LinkedIn group.

Chapter 8 Activities

1. Create a Presentation
   a. Create a class presentation using Keynote or PowerPoint.
   b. Post it in a location that you can access from your iPad.
2. Create a custom iBook application for your students using iBook Author.
3. Create an iPad course for your students using iTunes U Course Manager.
4. Develop a lesson plan for integrating one or more student music apps from this chapter.
5. Create a plan for integrating technology with the iPad in your music curriculum. Reference one or more of the books listed in this chapter.

Summary

This chapter focused on the impact that the iPad is having on music instruction. It included some of the many ways teachers can use the iPad as a teaching tool in the classroom and rehearsal and some of the many ways the iPad can be used by students. Students can use the iPad as a tool for learning about music and as an instrument to create and perform music. The iPad can also be an extremely portable and effective assessment tool for practice and performance. There are many support groups that can be joined and accessed for additional information.

Chapter 9
Music and More

Smartphones and tablets give you the power of a computer and Internet access in the palm of your hand. They provide a limitless range of applications for virtually any purpose. This chapter explores some essential tools and fun apps that can assist and entertain you.

Essential Tools

Calculator Apps

There is a calculator app on the iPad that will help with basic math, such as calculating how much memory a five-minute track consisting of eight tracks of audio will take up on your iPad.

Times Calc by Marco Po (Free)

https://itunes.apple.com/us/app/times-calc/id502386716?mt=8

Adding up song times when constructing a set list or computing album total time is just the sort of task that Times Calc, a time calculation app, handles with ease.

Figure 9.1. Times Calc.

Backline Calc by Audiofile Engineering (Free)

www.audiofile-engineering.com/backlinemobile/

The ultimate music calculator is an iPhone app that handles all of the calculations that Time Calc does, with additional features including calculations for acoustics and synching to picture. Functions are categorized by Length, Pitch, Timecode, Electric, Acoustics, and Files. Select the desired function in the list to display the appropriate calculator.

Figure 9.2. Backline Calc Select.

Figure 9.3. Backline Calc Calc.

Flashlight

One of the most useful apps to have both on a smartphone and the iPad is a flashlight app. There are many of them in the App Store, several of which are free including one that comes with iOS7.

Flashlight by iHandy Inc. (Free)

https://itunes.apple.com/us/app/flashlight-o/id381471023?mt=8

If you have an iPhone with the LED camera flash, be sure to download one of the apps that illuminates the LED. This provides a more focused beam of light and makes the phone easier to grasp when crawling in behind an equipment rack or navigating a dark stage, not to mention if the van breaks down on the way home from the gig.

Torchlight ◎ LED for iPhone 5 & 4 by Just2Me (Free)

https://itunes.apple.com/us/app/torchlight-led-for-iphone-5-4/id390019536?mt=8

> **Tip:** Don't forget the Camera app that comes with the iPad! Use it to document stage setups, mixer or effects settings, lighting, and yes, to take pictures with important people after the gig. It also can work for taking pictures of handwritten notes, phone numbers, business cards, receipts, driving directions, or anything else that usually gets lost by the time you need it. And in a pinch, if you need a piece of music in your music reader app (see chapter 4), you could take a photo of each page of the score.

Tour Support

If you are on the road frequently, there are a few apps to lend a hand with getting there and back. If you're a global traveler, you are probably familiar with Web-based services such as Priceline, Travelocity, Orbitz, and Kayak. These services also have free apps that will allow you to access your account and arrangements on the road. Many airlines also have apps that allow you to check schedules, book travel, and track your frequent flyer accounts. If you use these services frequently, the apps are a nice convenience. There are a few other apps that are essential to help the traveling or touring musician get from point A to point B smoothly.

My TSA by Transportation Security Administration (Free)

https://itunes.apple.com/us/app/my-tsa/id380200364?mt=8

If you spend even a little time traveling through airports, My TSA is for you. It provides you with approximate wait times for security screening lines in your departure airport, as well as information on flight delays at airports across the country. The app also has weather information for US airports to give you a heads-up on possible delays. You can use it to help determine if specific items are permissible in carry-on luggage and what items are restricted or may only be included in limited quantities.

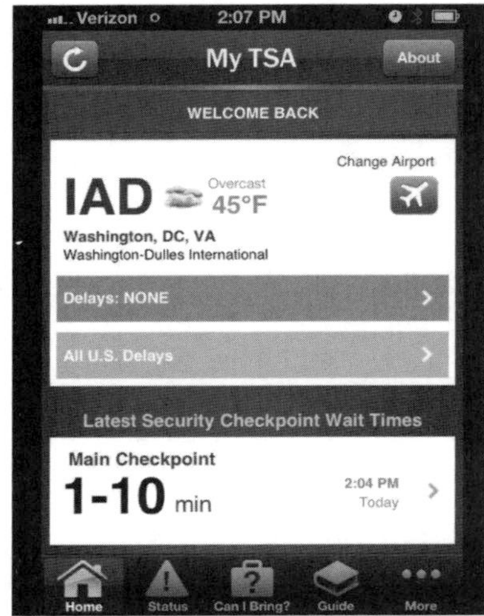

Figure 9.4. TSA 1.

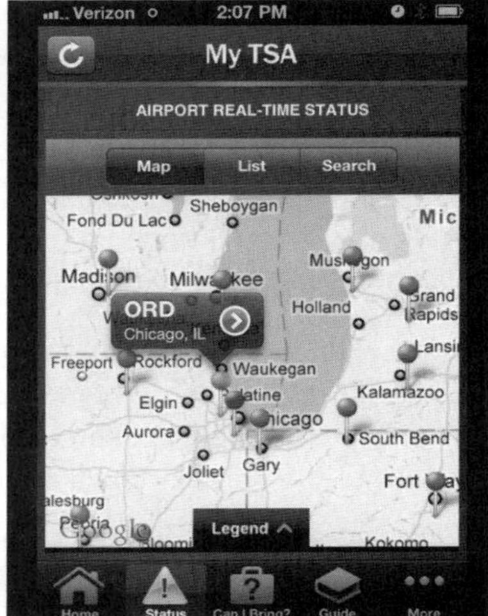

Figure 9.5. TSA 2.

Beat the Traffic by Triangle Software LLC (Free/In-App Purchases Available)

www.beatthetraffic.com/downloads.html

If traffic is a concern in getting to your gigs, consider a traffic app to scout your routes before leaving to find out if allowing more time is necessary or an alternate route might save you time.

Figure 9.6. Traffic.

Tip: If you are on the road a lot, there are apps for traffic information, places to eat, finding hotels, and getting roadside assistance. Don't forget to log your mileage—and of course, there are apps for that too.

TripLog: GPS Mileage Tracker by eSocial (Free/In-App Purchases)

https://itunes.apple.com/us/app/triplog-gps-mileage-tracker/id585918522?mt=8

When income-tax time rolls around, the miles you drove for business will need to be accounted for. The TripLog app uses GPS to track your trip. Enter your gas purchases if you want to track your miles per gallon. You can also enter any parking fees and tolls. Receipts can be recorded via the camera and uploaded to a secure location in the cloud. Then you can easily generate accurate expense reports. Using the report and cloud service requires an in-app subscription purchase.

Tip: If your iPad is Wi-Fi, install the traffic and TripLog apps on your iPhone.

Band Manager by Nathaniel Doe ($1.99)

www.nathanieldoe.com/

There is the music business, and there's the business of music. This app helps you track the business side of your musical life. It tracks income by gig and tour schedule, and it can provide directions to the venue.

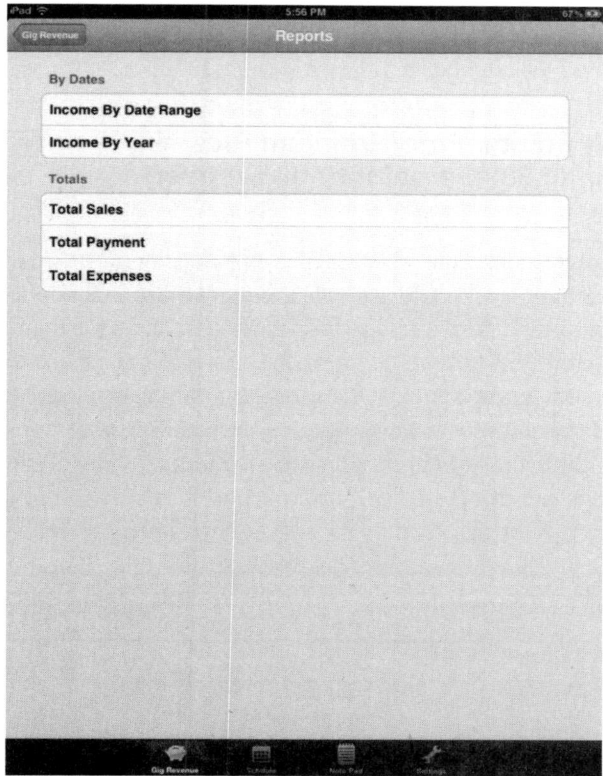

Figure 9.7.

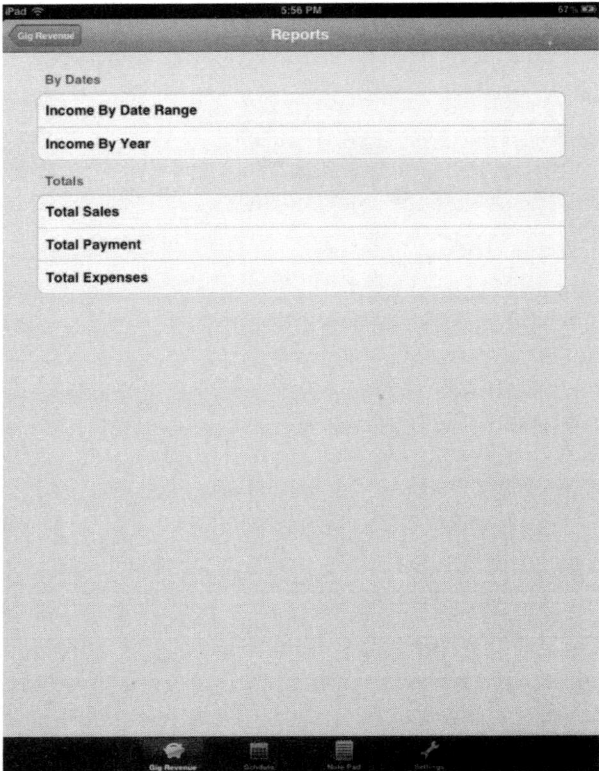

Figure 9.8.

Master Tour by Eventric
(Subscription Required. Premium: Free/Premium Plus: $9.99 per month per user/Professional: $39.99 per month per user)

www.eventric.com/Master-Tour/master-tour

For touring acts that use Eventric's Master Tour, there is an app extension of the Mac or PC desktop software. Tour managers, cast, and crew members can use this app to view and post all the details of a tour. Easily manage information such as passport data, per-diem rates, airline reservations, hotel bookings, directions to performance venues, comp lists, and media and business contacts. Touring gear can be catalogued to create manifests for tracking. Information such as stage size and loading access for over 5,000 venues worldwide can be accessed via the software's database. Tasks can be assigned and scheduled, set lists can be created and printed, and guest lists can be created and exported to the event box office. At the end of the day, expenses can be tallied, as well as tracking settlements, advances, promoter splits and income.

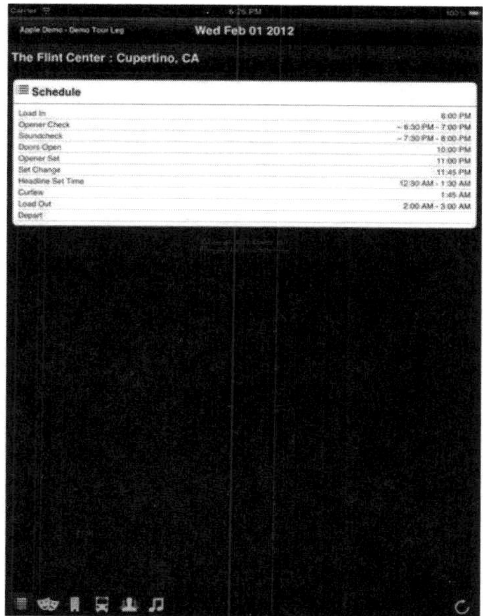

Figure 9.9.

Music Tools

Music Practice Tools by Capo
by SuperMegaUltraGroovy Inc. ($19.99)

http://supermegaultragroovy.com/products/Capo/iphone.html

Learning or transcribing a song is easier when you can slow down the speed of the track without changing the pitch. Capo can access any song in your iTunes library. You can select a passage to loop, isolate the left or right channel in mono to isolate specific parts, and then use the 10-band equalizer to further highlight the frequencies of the track you are trying to hear.

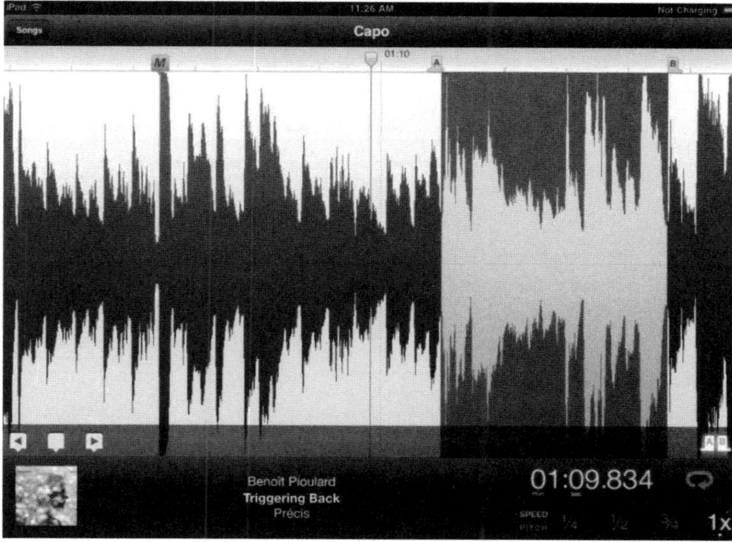

Figure 9.10.

VIDEO 9.1. MUSIC PRACTICE TOOLS DEMO.

Figure 9.11.
http://youtu.be/DiH8Rt424el

Jammit by Jammit (Free/In-App Purchase by Song Required)

www.jammit.com/

Jammit is the app portal of the www.jammit.com website that takes the music-minus-one concept to a new level. If you're a singer, guitarist, bassist, keyboardist, or drummer, Jammit allows you to learn, play along, and then replace your respective part in a growing list of rock, pop, country, and jazz recordings. You can record the results and export them via e-mail or to Facebook.

Figure 9.12.

VIDEO 9.2. JAMMIT.

Figure 9.13.
http://youtu.be/578gRFgauls

Alfred Play Along by Jammit (Free/In-App Purchase by Song Required)

https://itunes.apple.com/us/app/alfred-play-along/id602776576?mt=8

This app is similar to Jammit, above, but for players of band and orchestra instruments. The library of songs is smaller and more diverse. There are pop hits from Led Zeppelin to Michael Jackson, traditional hymns, and selections from Harry Potter soundtracks and the World of Warcraft video-game score.

Figure 9.14.

VIDEO 9.3 ALFRED PLAY ALONG.

Figure 9.15.
http://youtu.be/RZDbSe7eX3Y

Music Recognition Software

If you've ever had a tune stuck in your head and couldn't think of the title, or heard a song used on TV or in a film and wanted to know what song or artist it was, then you need music-recognition software.

SoundHound by SoundHound Inc. (Free)

www.soundhound.com/index.php?action=s.home

SoundHound can recognize songs by "listening" to the track through the built-in iPad microphone. You can also sing or hum into the microphone if the track is not available, but taking your iPad into the shower, where you may sound your best, is not recommended! You can also type or speak lyrics to identify songs. When SoundHound identifies a track, it provides a link to the iTunes track. SoundHound will access its lyric database and provide, when available, scrolling lyrics to the identified song. SoundHound can also access and play your iTunes library like the music app described in chapter 1.

Artist Apps

Jorden Rudess is not the only artist who has contributed to the iPad app world. Artists are using apps in different ways: some as extensions of their websites, others to make artistic statements, and for rock icons George Harrison and John Lennon, as a way of documenting a few small bits of their legacy.

The Rolling Stones, Madonna, Red Hot Chili Peppers, and Bon Jovi are just some of the artists who have apps that provide fans with tour dates, product release dates, photos, lyrics, and exclusive content.

MusicTiles by Entertainment Robotics ($2.99/In-App Purchases Required for Full-Length Tracks)

www.musictiles.com/

Tracks from Peter Gabriel's album *So* have been incorporated into an app called MusicTiles. The interface consists of a grid with tiles, each representing an instrument or group of instruments on a specific track. You can create your own mix of the song by rearranging the tiles on the screen, changing the element's position in the stereo field, and dropping parts in and out as the song plays.

You can record and save your remixes inside the app and e-mail the results to yourself or friends and family, or share with the world by e-mailing to share@musictiles.com. This is a great app for analyzing mixing as well as the musical elements of each track.

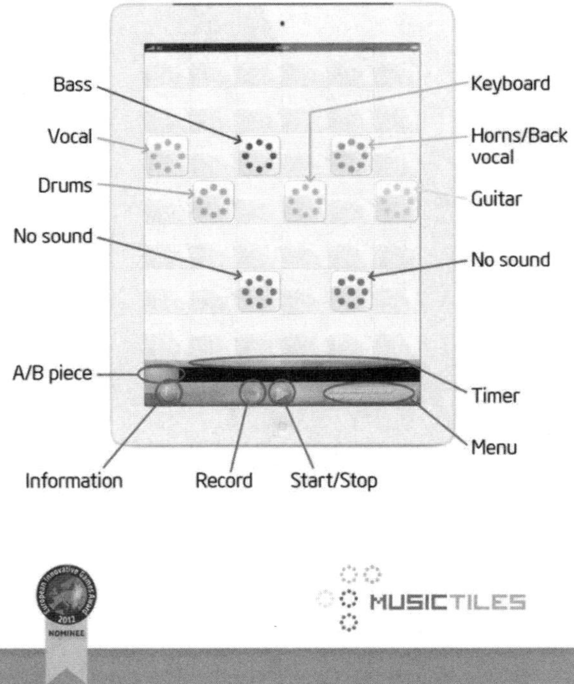

Figure 9.16.

VIDEO 9.4. MUSIC TILES.

Figure 9.17.
http://youtu.be/9A2XXXBA35E

Scape by Opal LTD ($5.99)

www.generativemusic.com/scape.html

Scape is the latest in a series of apps from ambient-music artist Brian Eno and the first of his to be made exclusively for iPad. Eno's previous iOS apps—Boom, Trope and Air—treated the app as a long-form creative work.

Users create in Scape by first selecting a background sound, which plays constantly, and then adding notes and phrases. The sound texture can be varied by adding moods that alter the colors of the background. The app starts with a basic sound set, but the more you use it, the more sounds become available, adding a gamelike aspect to this very visual app.

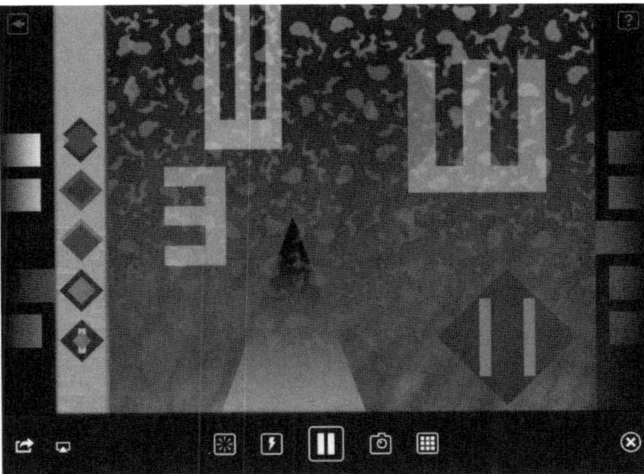

Figure 9.18.

VIDEO 9.5 SCAPE.

Figure 9.19.
http://youtu.be/8zNLIKRrUVk

Björk Biophilia by Björk ($12.99)

http://bjork.com/

Björk has collaborated with several artists and app designers to create this app based on her *Biophilia* album. The journey into this immersive world begins with a 3-D galaxy view accompanied by the song "Cosmogony." All songs in the collection have interactive art, music notation, MIDI data, lyrics, and essays that explore their inspiration. This is a unique achievement, both as an app and as an artistic statement.

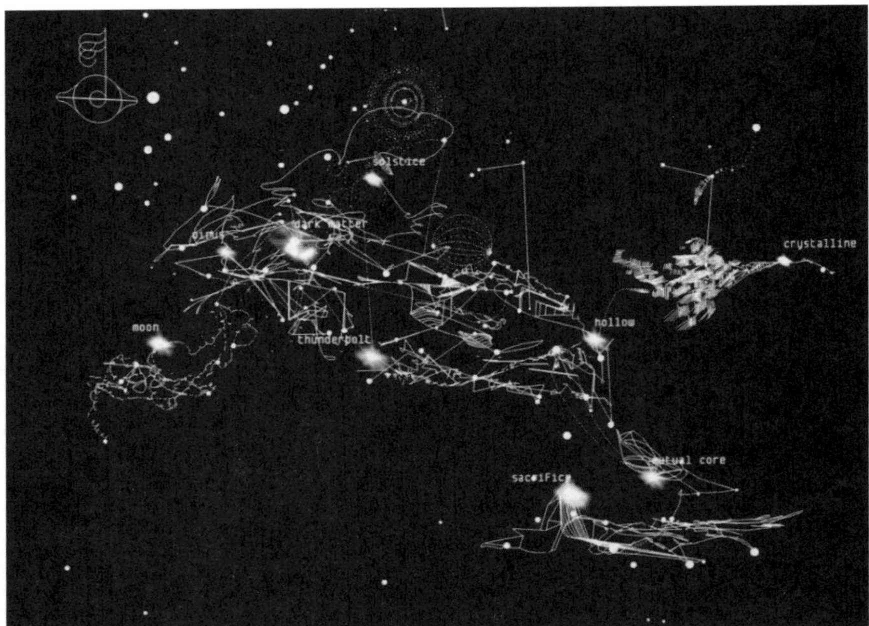

Figure 9.20.

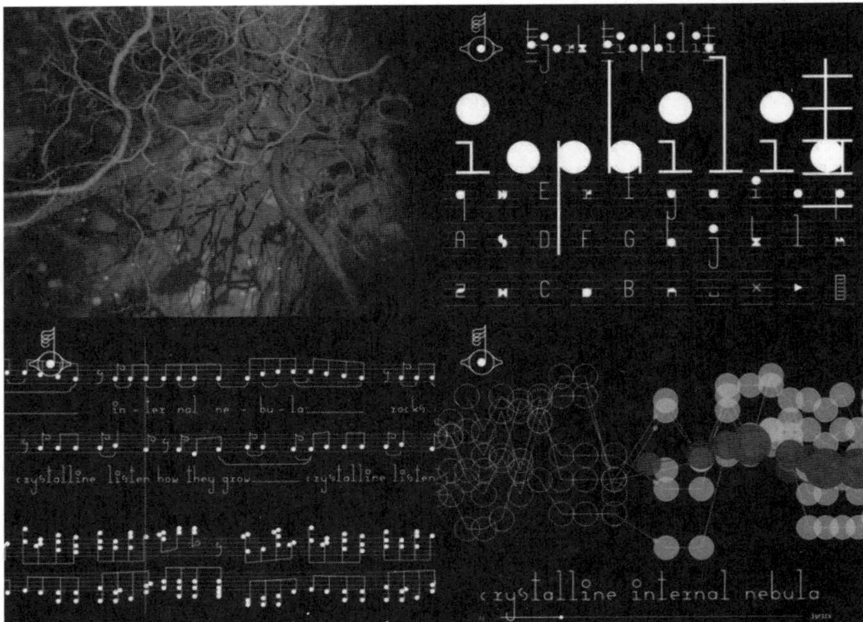

Figure 9.21.

VIDEO 9.6. BJORK.

Figure 9.22.
http://youtu.be/n8c0x6dO2bg

The John Lennon Letters by Hachette UK (LBS) ($8.99)

https://itunes.apple.com/us/app/the-john-lennon-letters/id579613944?mt=8

This app is designed to add additional content to the Hunter Davies book *The John Lennon Letters.* The app includes audio of the letters read by Christopher Eccleston, as well as some audio by the author.

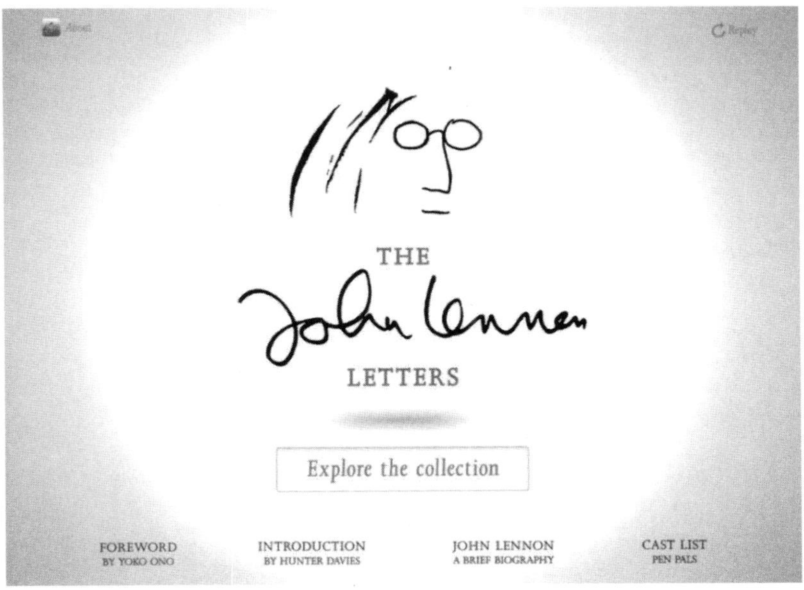

Figure 9.23.

The Guitar Collection: George Harrison by Bandwidth ($9.99)

https://itunes.apple.com/us/app/guitar-collection-george-harrison/id499105381?mt=8

If you are a guitar geek, this app is a must-have. It catalogs the guitars from the collection of George Harrison. Included are detailed hi-res photographs, 360-degree views, and recordings of Harrison introducing and demonstrating the tone of some of the instruments in the collection. The company promises future free updates adding more guitars from the collection.

Figure 9.24.

Entertaining Family Members of All Ages

Every musician sooner or later encounters the family gathering where you are called on to impress the assembled with "something musical." Always keep an app or three handy for this purpose. You may find some entertainment value in other apps found in this book, but here are some specifically designed for entertainment and just plain fun for family members of all ages.

Singing Fingers by Beginner's Mind (Free)

http://singingfingers.com/

This app combines finger painting and sampling to produce sound. Sing, play an instrument, talk, or record whatever sound you want, and while recording, draw a shape on the screen to which Singing Fingers will attach the sound recorded.

Sounds are performed by touching and/or sliding your fingers along the shapes drawn while recording. You can have multiple samples on the screen at the same time, so you can create your own "band."

Figure 9.25.

VIDEO 9.7 SINGING FINGERS.

Figure 9.26.
http://youtu.be/iCYA7N-vdZA

Music Matching with Lisa Loeb— a tile-matching game by Gabuduck (Free)

www.gabuduck.com/

Music Matching adds a musical element to the basic matching game. Each tile has an instrument in the graphic, and the instrument sound associated with it plays when you select the tile. There are three difficulty levels to choose from.

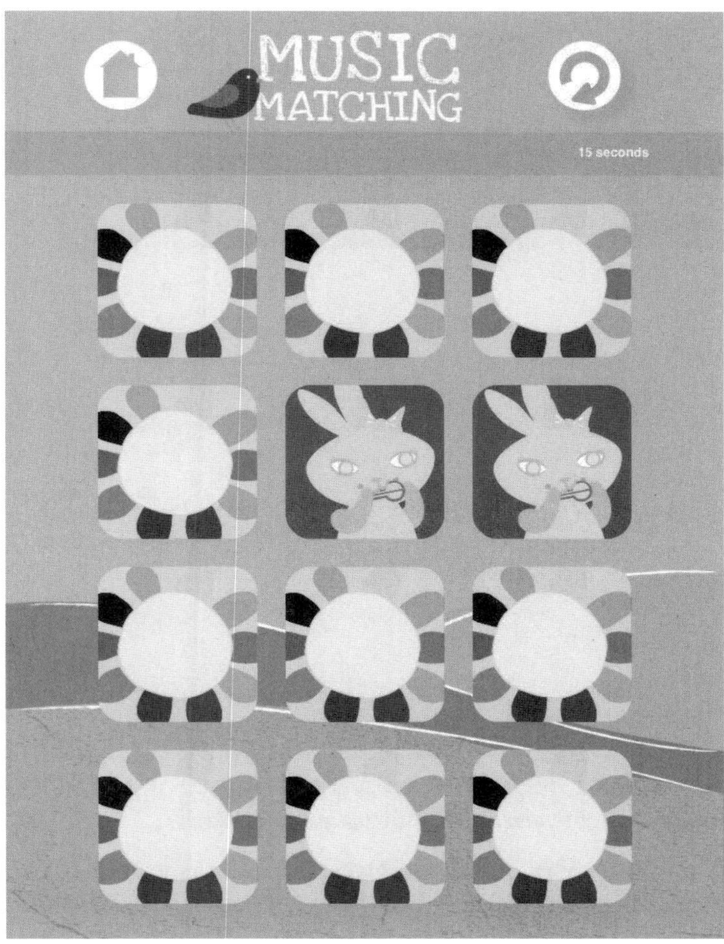

Figure 9.27.

Toca Band by Toca Boca ($1.99)
http://tocaboca.com/

Toca Band has a group of characters, each playing a specific instrument; a three-level stage to place them on; and a song to play. Place a character on the front (green) row of the stage, and that character will begin playing his or her part. Move the character to the second (red) level, and the part becomes more complex. The third (blue) level produces a yet more complex part. Placing a character on the star platform allows the user to play a solo on that instrument by tapping on the screen. Choose and blend your ensemble; then rock the house with a solo.

Figure 9.28.

VIDEO 9.8 TOCA BAND.

Figure 9.29.
http://youtu.be/MN1nv9PIkxI

Groovemaker Free for iPad, IK Multimedia (Free)
www.ikmultimedia.com/products/cat-view.php?C=family-groovemaker

Should your audience be a little older, try Groovemaker, and let them select drum, bass, and pad elements to create their own mixes. You can purchase additional packs for different musical styles.

Figure 9.30.

VIDEO 9.9 GROOVE MAKER.

Figure 9.31.
http://youtu.be/fllKssjbr2w

CineBeat by Smule (Free/In-App Purchases)

www.smule.com/cinebeat/

Create a music video on the fly with CineBeat. Record up to 15 seconds of video in the app; then turn it into a music video. You can also use photos and video already in your iPad, and the app will work its magic with filters that mimic different musical and visual styles. Share your video with the world via Facebook, Twitter, e-mail, or SMS.

VIDEO 9.10. CINEBEAT.

Figure 9.32.
http://youtu.be/sNMejxqD1vo

Angry Birds by Rovio Entertainment Ltd. ($0.99)

https://itunes.apple.com/us/app/angry-birds-hd-free/id409809295?mt=8

When all else fails, pop those piggies! Then use some of the apps mentioned in previous chapters to record a cover of the theme song. Here's some inspiration.

VIDEO 9.11. ANGRY BIRDS.

Figure 9.33.
http://youtu.be/7UCm6uyzNE8

Tip: If you become obsessed with any noisemaking app, revisit the section on volume control in chapter 1.

One App to Create Them All

Xcode by Apple Inc. (Free from the Macintosh App Store)

www.macupdate.com/app/mac/13621/apple-xcode

If anything in this book has inspired you to tackle the task of app creation on your own, and you own a Macintosh desktop or laptop computer, downloading the Xcode app is the first step of the journey. Xcode is used to create applications for Mac OS, as well as for iOS devices. Apple also offers a free tutorial app that is available in the Macintosh App Store.

To help you further explore the process of app creation, there are Web classes available in iTunes U (see chapter 8) or books you can purchase in the iTunes book store. Once your app is ready to test, you'll need to join the iOS Developer Program. The fee to enroll in this program is $99 per year, and it is required to get your app through the testing and submission process. With a little marketing savvy, you might make the $99 investment some of the best money spent, by providing fans exclusives through your app that cannot be found anywhere else.

Oh, One More Thing

The iPad Commode Caddy. Available Online ($39.99).
Okay, everyone, make up your own joke here (but you know you want one).

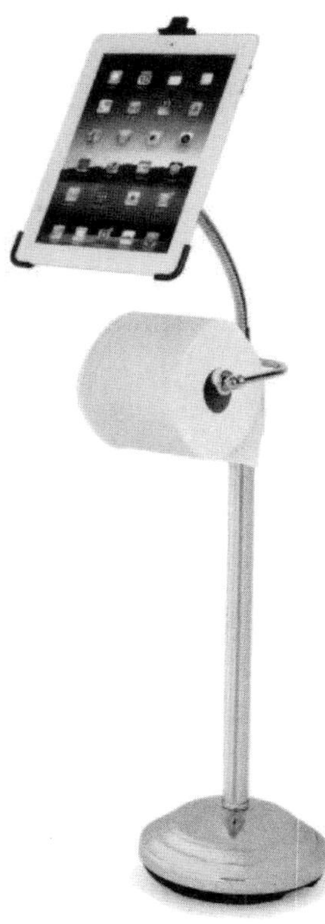

Figure 9.34.

Chapter 9 Activities

1. Use an app to map out your next gig and record the expenses.
2. Search for your favorite artist apps.
3. Organize a game of "Name That Tune" and use the song recognition app as needed.
4. Create your own music video with CineBeat.
5. Create your own custom app with Xcode.

Summary

The apps in this chapter are a sample of the vast variety that are waiting to be discovered. By the time you read this, there will be even more from which to choose. The categories include essential tools, calculators for musicians, tour support and management, fun practice tools, artist apps, and apps for just plain fun. We also touched on what you need to do in order to create your own apps.

Index

About the Authors

Producer and composer Vincent A. Leonard Jr. has had works premiered nationally and internationally. He is published by Arrangers Publishing Company, Educational Programs Publications, and National Music Works. He is coauthor of *Recording in the Digital World, Finale: An Easy Guide to Music Notation,* and *Sibelius: A Comprehensive Guide to Music Notation.* In 1996, he and fellow producer and engineer Jack Klotz Jr. formed Invinceable Entertainment, from which they have released two CDs, *Magic Up Our Sleeve* and *On the Brink of Tomorrow.* Leonard's compositional credits include theme and episode music for the *Captain Courteous* radio series, numerous theater pieces, and industrials. He has provided orchestrations for world-premier productions of *Redwall* for Opera Delaware, as well as *Elliot and the Magic Bed, Isabell and the Pretty Ugly Spell,* and *The Little Princess* for Upper Darby Summer Stage. Also widely known as a copyist and arranger, he has worked on projects with Peter Nero, the Philly Pops Orchestra, Doc Severinsen, the London Symphony Orchestra, Chuck Mangione, and Leslie Burrs, and on musicals by Duke Ellington, Alan Menken, Kurt Weil, and Mitch Leigh. Leonard is a member of NARAS and ASCAP, and he is active as a clinician and beta tester for music software for Macintosh computers.

Thomas Rudolph, Ed.D., is an adjunct instructor for Berklee Online. He also conducts summer workshops in music technology at Villanova University and Central Connecticut State University. Dr. Rudolph is one of the seminal people in music technology. He began his work as a clinician and workshop leader in the field in 1982. In addition to his work in music technology, Dr. Rudolph is a busy trumpet player in the Philadelphia area and performs with the group Gaudeamus. His compositions and arrangements have been published by Neil Kjos and Northeastern Music Publications Inc. Dr. Rudolph has authored and coauthored many books, including: *Finale: An Easy Guide to Music Notation, Sibelius: A Comprehensive Guide to Sibelius Music Notation Software, Teaching Music with Technology,* and *Recording in the Digital World: YouTube in Music Education and Finding Funds for Music Technology.* He was one of four coauthors of the TI:ME publication *Technology Strategies for Music Education.* Dr. Rudolph is coauthor of the Alfred Music Tech Series, which includes *Playing Keyboard, Music Production and MIDI Sequencing,* and *Composing with Notation Software.* He has published many articles on music technology that have appeared in the *Music Educators Journal, The Instrumentalist,* and *Downbeat* magazine.